First Certificate in English Practice

Ona Low

Edward Arnold

© Ona Low 1983

First published 1977
by Edward Arnold (Publishers) Ltd
41 Bedford Square, London WC1B 3DQ

Edward Arnold (Australia) Pty Ltd,
80 Waverley Road, Caulfield East,
Victoria 3145, Australia

Reprinted 1978, 1979, 1980, 1982
Second ('Revised') edition 1983
Reprinted 1983, 1984, 1986

British Library Cataloguing in Publication Data

Low, Ona
   First certificate in English practice.—2nd ed.
   1. English language—Text-books for foreigners
   I. Title
   428.2′4   PE1128

ISBN 0-7131-8148-6

All Rights Reserved. No part of this publication may be reproduced, stored in a retrieval system, or transmitted in any form or by any means, electronic, mechanical, photocopying, recording or otherwise, without the prior permission of Edward Arnold (Publishers) Ltd.

By the same author
First Certificate in English Practice KEY
Proficiency in English Practice, and KEY
First Certificate in English Course, and KEY
Proficiency in English Course, and KEY
Speak English Fluently: Book 1
Speak English Fluently: Book 2

Text set in 10/11pt English Times Compugraphic
by Colset Private Limited, Singapore
Printed and bound by Thomson Litho Ltd,
East Kilbride, Scotland

Preface

First Certificate in English Practice is intended to supplement *First Certificate Course*. While the main purpose of the latter is to cover in some detail the teaching material which will ensure comprehensive preparation for the First Certificate examination, this text provides practice in answering the various types of questions most likely to appear on the examination papers together with advice about how to deal with these.

The material presented in *First Certificate in English Practice* is determined by the examination syllabus and while all of it is original, the questions and exercises are closely modelled on those of the three written papers included in the examination, on the Listening Comprehension texts and responses and on the requirements of the three parts of the Interview. The overall standard is that of the examination and, with some exceptions, the vocabulary is to be found in the Cambridge English Lexicon.

In certain cases, above all when class meetings are restricted to four hours or less weekly, *First Certificate Course* may prove too comprehensive for adequate coverage of its contents in the time available. If the students' language ability approaches already that required to achieve a satisfactory examination standard, *First Certificate in English Practice* may provide a useful replacement for the course book. Preparation for the examination will then consist mainly of familiarising students with the kind of question to be expected and the most effective way of answering it, the teacher making good any language deficiencies as they are exposed.

Preface to the Second Edition

Adaptations have been made to include the new types of material appearing on the modified papers and questions which form part of the 1984 Syllabus.

This edition includes advice on dealing effectively with the Reading Comprehension, Use of English and Listening Comprehension papers and the three sections of the Interview.

Examples of a letter, composition expressing opinions and a speech are given, together with an example of the kind of continuous writing exercise required in Use of English Section B.

The Listening Comprehension texts are not normally available to students; the transcripts are therefore published in *First Certificate in English Practice Key,* together with the answers to all the exercises in this book.

I should like to thank John Millerchip of the British Centre, Venice for his help and encouragement in producing this book, and my students for acting as guinea pigs.

Contents

Preface		iii
Summary of the requirements of the 1984 Syllabus		5
Paper 1	**Reading Comprehension**	7
Section A:	Graded groups 1–10	8
	Ungraded groups A–E	14
Section B:	Group 1 Narrative passages	23
	Group 2 Informative passages	30
	Group 3 Public notices, instructions, advertisements etc.	34
Paper 2	**Composition**	40
	Introduction — some suggestions for effective writing	40
	Letter-writing	41
	Sample letter	
	Description	42
	Narrative	43
	Expression of opinions	43
	Sample composition	
	A talk or speech	44
	Sample composition	
	Prescribed texts	45
Paper 3	**Use of English**	47
Section A:	English usage exercises	48
Section B:	Recording and interpreting information	66
Paper 4	**Listening Comprehension**	73
Paper 5	**Interview**	87
Section A:	Conversation based on photographs	87
Section B:	Interpretation of situations from passages to be read aloud	97
Section C:	Structured communication exercises	101

Acknowledgements

The publishers would like to thank the following for permission to reproduce copyright material:

Her Majesty's Stationery Office for an extract from *Higher Education — Finding your Way* reproduced by permission of the Controller of HMSO, p. 32; Manpower Services Commission for part of their Employment Services Division leaflet EP1 72, p. 34 and The Royal Society for the Prevention of Accidents for part of their leaflet RS MCY 21 Ride Well Ride Safely, p. 36.

For copyright illustrations: COI, Crown Copyright Reserved: p. 95; Diana Lanham: p. 89; David Richardson: p. 90; John Walmsley: p. 91; Henry Grant: p. 92; Antony McAvoy: pp. 93, 94 & 96.

A summary of the requirements of the 1984 syllabus

Paper 1: Reading Comprehension   (1 hour)   40 marks

Section A

A gap-filling exercise consisting of 25 sentences each followed by four words or phrases from which one must be selected for completion of the foregoing sentence.
(One mark is awarded for each correct answer)

Section B

Three or more passages with a total of 15 multiple choice items related to them. Each item will consist of a question with a choice of four answers or an unfinished statement with a choice of four endings designed to test comprehension of the passage before it.

The emphasis of the items related to the first passage will be on gist comprehension of the passage, and items throughout Section B will also test comprehension of specific information points. The third passage and the items on it will test understanding of advertising material, public notices, operating instructions etc., and will not usually take the form of continuous prose.
(Two marks are awarded for each correct answer)

Paper 2: Composition   (1½ hours)   40 marks

The writing of two compositions, each between 120 and 180 words, chosen from a list of possible topics, usually five in number. The topics may require a letter, description, narrative, expression of opinion, speech, or answer to a question on one of a number of prescribed texts.

Paper 3: Use of English   (2 hours)   40 marks

Section A

A number of exercises (usually four) each comprising a number of discrete items testing the candidate's knowledge of English language usage in controlled contexts. The exercises may include:
— a gap-filling exercise based on a passage containing (often 20) completion items, involving structural rather than vocabulary considerations
— a transformation exercise involving tense, prepositional usage, word order etc., as applied to sentences

The exercises may also include:
- word formation, usually necessitating the transformation of a word used as one part of speech to another e.g. verb to noun form
- the construction of sentences from given elements to form a letter
- dialogue sequences involving the construction of question forms
- conversion from direct to reported speech and vice versa
- choice of vocabulary or structure within given areas of association

Section B

The writing of a continuous prose passage based on the candidate's interpretation of information presented in one of a variety of forms including notes, lists, instructions, visual material such as graphs or charts etc.
(An average of 15 marks per exercise is awarded)

Paper 4: Listening Comprehension (approx. 30 minutes)
20 marks

Suitable responses to questions on a recorded series of texts. The questions may be of varying kinds involving selection or recording of material presented, labelling of pictures, gap-filling and multiple-choice responses. The texts will include radio-type sequences of news or features, situational dialogues, announcements etc.

Paper 5: Interview (20 minutes)
40 marks

A A conversation with the examiner of about 5 minutes relating to a picture which has been handed to the candidate.
B After a few moments for preparation, the identification of the probable speech situation referred to in a short passage and the reading aloud of the passage.
C A structured communication exercise involving one of the following:
- a short talk (with possible discussion) based on a prepared topic
- the discussion of a set book (if one has been studied)
- extended situational responses
- opinions and definitions
- the eliciting of information
- problem solving

Paper 1   Reading Comprehension

This paper is in two parts, Section A and Section B. For each question you answer correctly in Section A, you gain one mark; for each question you answer correctly in Section B you gain two marks. No marks are deducted for wrong answers.

Answer all the questions. Indicate your choice of answer in every case on the separate answer sheet which should show your name and examination index number. Follow carefully the instructions about how to record your answer.

Section A

In this section you must choose the word or phrase which best completes the sentence.

General advice

While the choice of words in this section depends to some extent on word meaning alone, other structural and grammatical factors may influence the selection.

Here is a summary of some of the considerations you should bear in mind when making your choice. Reference is made to sentences which illustrate the point in question.

1. Distinction between words which have some kind of relationship but only one of which would fit meaningfully into the given sentence. Careful consideration of the meaning of the sentence has to be given here.
   e.g. Group 1: 1, 2, 3.

2. Distinction between words which have some similarity in meaning.
   e.g. Group 3: 1, 2, 3; Group C: 3, 4, 5.

3. Distinction between words that may be confused because of a similarity in form of one of them to a word in another language, though the two words are different in meaning in English.
   e.g. Group 3: 6 (bored/annoyed); Group A: 5 (sensible/sensitive).

4. A word selection determined by a preposition in the sentence.
   e.g. Group C: 16 (reason for).

5. The countability or uncountability of a noun as indicated by the inclusion or omission of the indefinite article in the sentence.
   e.g. Group E: 16 (a suggestion).

6. Particles used after phrasal verbs.
   e.g. Group 2: 2.

7   Selection of a word that is related to a verbal construction in the sentence.
     e.g.   Group 7: 8 (a clause follows).
            Group B: 13 (an infinitive follows).

8   Selection of a suitable verb tense.
     e.g.   Group A: 1 (modal form and tense).
            Group 4: 8 (influence of reported speech).

Exercises

Groups 1–10 are graded in difficulty.

Group 1

1 Some town children never saw grass or trees and could play only in a small _____.
   A field   **B** garden   **C** yard   **D** park

2 We arrived at the _____ very late when everybody there was already asleep.
   A camp   **B** office   **C** station   **D** restaurant

3 He hung up his overcoat in the _____ as soon as he came into the house.
   A cellar   **B** attic   **C** hall   **D** ground floor

4 You'll be _____ your money if you buy that dress: you'll never wear it.
   A spending   **B** wasting   **C** giving away   **D** losing

5 The _____ between England and France can be very rough.
   A passage   **B** crossing   **C** travel   **D** drive

6 I _____ up before six o'clock this morning.
   A stood   **B** got   **C** rose   **D** awoke

7 It was very _____ of you to give me a lift.
   A useful   **B** friendly   **C** grateful   **D** kind

8 _____ you don't hurry, you'll miss the train.
   A when   **B** if   **C** as   **D** even if

9 I'm trying _____ to get this sentence right.
   A hardly   **B** well   **C** hard   **D** very much

10 He turned up his _____ to protect his neck from the wind.
   A collar   **B** sleeve   **C** cap   **D** scarf

Group 2

1 You should always keep your valuable jewellery in a _____.
   A drawer   **B** wardrobe   **C** cupboard   **D** safe

2 The police are looking _____ the strange disappearance of the bank manager.
   A at   **B** for   **C** into   **D** over

3 _____ grows only in a hot climate.
   A silk   **B** wool   **C** cotton   **D** linen

4 Light _____ will be served during the interval.
   A food   B meal   C drinks   D refreshments

5 He thinks all animal food is harmful so he lives on bread, vegetables and _____.
   A eggs   B cheese   C beans   D fruit

6 My brother went to Norway _____ and will return in four years' time.
   A two years ago   B two years past   C for two years   D before two years

7 The swimming-pool is so _____ that it's safe for small children.
   A calm   B flat   C shallow   D smooth

8 Miss Keen, a highly-qualified _____, answers all the manager's letters.
   A typewriter   B clerk   C secretary   D reporter

9 A black cat was sitting on the river _____ watching the fishermen.
   A coast   B shore   C bank   D border

10 _____ we get some rain soon, there will be little fruit this summer.
   A if   B in case   C unless   D provided

Group 3

1 The tourists are looking for holiday souvenirs to _____ home with them.
   A bring   B take   C fetch   D take away

2 A dog can be a very pleasant _____ on long country walks.
   A friend   B fellow   C companion   D company

3 People were walking slowly under the trees on either side of the broad _____ through the park.
   A alley   B track   C way   D avenue

4 If you'd only telephoned, I shouldn't have been so _____ about you.
   A preoccupied   B upset   C nervous   D worried

5 Many elderly people find painting pictures a relaxing and enjoyable _____.
   A job   B employment   C work   D occupation

6 Half the students were yawning as they were _____ with the lesson.
   A tired   B bored   C uninterested   D annoyed

7 He always seems _____, never complaining about his many troubles.
   A careless   B merry   C cheerful   D glad

8 Climbing boots provide support for the wearer's _____.
   A knees   B ankles   C toes   D elbows

9 The scheme has been introduced to encourage people to _____ money for their old age.
   A save   B spare   C give away   D preserve

10 I can't let you have this _____ it isn't mine to give.
  A provided   B for   C though   D while

Group 4

1 You can get drinking water by turning this _____.
  A switch   B pipe   C knob   D tap

2 You were _____ to get that ticket as it was the last one left.
  A happy   B lucky   C willing   D grateful

3 Little Kevin gets on well with his grandfather in spite of the age _____ between them.
  A space   B division   C separation   D gap

4 The lorry was carrying a _____ of potatoes.
  A pile   B load   C charge   D lump

5 Among other things the Town _____ is responsible for parks, fire services, refuse collection and libraries.
  A Committee   B Authority   C Community   D Council

6 The children enjoyed _____ their father in sand so that only his head was visible.
  A enclosing   B hiding   C burying   D rolling

7 Practice and experience in driving in traffic will make you a much more _____ driver.
  A conscious   B confident   C sure   D certain

8 He asked his boss whether he _____ have time off to visit his wife in hospital.
  A may   B might   C can   D should

9 He refuses to go to France by boat and won't fly _____ so he'll just have to stay in England.
  A either   B also   C neither   D else

10 The car stopped so _____ that the one behind almost ran into it.
  A immediately   B closely   C soon   D suddenly

Group 5

1 The senior accounts clerk has been _____ for dishonesty.
  A put out   B dismissed   C resigned   D retired

2 A new writer of plays often pays a(n) _____ to persuade someone to produce it.
  A agent   B actor   C representative   D manager

3 As he moved farther into the cave, he noticed that the water was moving _____ and not towards the open air.
  A inside   B inwards   C within   D outwards

4 Immediately the radio message was received, three ships changed their _____ and made their way towards the sinking vessel.
  A crossing   B course   C journey   D passage

5 The salt that can be dug out of the ground is a _____.
A metal   B material   C mineral   D substance

6 The light gradually _____ and shapes and colours grew fainter.
A melted   B disappeared   C faded   D died

7 It is quite _____ for you to have an immediate operation.
A essential   B definite   C certain   D decided

8 In the sunlight each waterdrop shone like the clearest _____
A crystal   B silver   C pearl   D mirror

9 The nurse told me that Daniel's _____ immediately after his operation was satisfactory.
A condition   B situation   C state   D health

10 He has visited many countries but says he has not found a really honest man _____.
A anywhere   B wherever   C somewhere   D nowhere

Group 6

1 The white _____ found in south-west England is used for making plates and dishes.
A soil   B sand   C earth   D clay

2 This peculiar watermark is a sure _____ that the notepaper was produced before 1900.
A record   B stamp   C signal   D sign

3 By now the fruit had become quite _____ and we had to get rid of it.
A ruined   B overripe   C rotten   D poisonous

4 Difficulties often _____ in keeping traffic moving after a heavy snowstorm.
A arise   B happen   C become   D appear

5 Must you _____ in other people's affairs?
A disturb   B interfere   C interrupt   D mix

6 I was only a little _____ to hear they had separated as I knew they often quarrelled.
A astonished   B surprised   C confused   D upset

7 The policeman made all the necessary enquiries about the accident and then wrote out his _____.
A information   B report   C results   D details

8 He is the _____ of the committee that arranges the club programme.
A president   B director   C chairman   D leader

9 The glasses were packed carefully so that there should be no _____ during the journey.
A accident   B theft   C breakage   D destruction

10 Everybody _____ him on the standard of his performance.
A cheered   B congratulated   C applauded   D clapped

Group 7

1. One of the _____ in the wheel was loose so it had to be tightened.
   A teeth   B frames   C nuts   D nails

2. Far from being rough when he played with smaller children, he was always surprisingly _____.
   A gentle   B sweet   C patient   D careful

3. He has lived at this _____ all his life.
   A neighbourhood   B district   C house   D address

4. The party admits it has done little about unemployment and this _____ must be discussed in detail very soon.
   A apology   B argument   C matter   D excuse

5. Before there were factories, people used to _____ wool into cloth in their own homes.
   A spin   B weave   C knit   D manufacture

6. This is a good _____ of his delight in unusual words and patterns.
   A passage   B example   C case   D expression

7. If our _____ development is to be encouraged, many machines in our factories must be replaced by more efficient ones.
   A industrial   B mechanical   C industrious   D practical

8. He said he would not _____ that I had accused him of cheating.
   A forget   B forgive   C pardon   D overlook

9. Most of the cattle are _____ under the trees.
   A lying   B laying   C remaining   D leaning

10. On leaving school he became an office-boy and having no _____ to rise higher, he only wasted his time.
    A ambition   B determination   C success   D purpose

Group 8

1. Short sight can be _____ by the use of suitable glasses.
   A fixed   B corrected   C improved   D reduced

2. Have you forgotten the _____ you made yesterday with my secretary to have the meeting in my office?
   A appointment   B arrangement   C decision   D suggestion

3. There was a sudden bright _____ of anger in his eyes as he listened to the soldier's report.
   A fire   B flame   C flash   D shadow

4. Many of those watching used handkerchiefs to _____ away the tears from their eyes.
   A wipe   B brush   C wash   D rub

5. When the owner let the house to me I signed a(n) _____ that I would leave at the end of December.
   A advice   B agreement   C bargain   D insurance

6 Whether or not you like some kinds of modern furniture is a matter of _____.
A comparison B favour C temperament D taste

7 He can hardly _____ having to accept orders from a man so much younger than himself.
A bear B suffer C resist D mind

8 The shopkeeper often checks his _____ to find out what to order.
A stocks B reserves C provisions D accounts

9 He is indeed too fat but _____ that he is an excellent dancer.
A in spite of B as well as C in contrast to
D owing to

10 The Government has expressed its _____ of the plan to build three new power stations.
A faith B trust C confidence D approval

Group 9

1 The sound of our voices was completely _____ by the roar of the machinery.
A reduced B scattered C decreased D drowned

2 He moved his glass violently as he spoke and some of the beer still remaining in it _____ on to the floor.
A overflowed B fell C poured D spilt

3 The scientist was studying the _____ of different kinds of insects in bright light.
A behaviour B treatment C character D conduct

4 They destroyed his home and his future but one day, he declares, he will _____ them suitably for what they have done.
A revenge B reward C repay D harm

5 The king had no _____ on any disloyal subject.
A sympathy B allowance C forgiveness D mercy

6 Early man used to _____ the sun, moon, trees and stones as his gods.
A consider B serve C worship D admire

7 In the Children's Home she has the _____ for looking after fifteen children.
A duty B responsibility C authority D care

8 The police are making very careful enquiries as this is clearly a(n) _____ of murder.
A accusation B case C circumstance D charge

9 As soon as he saw his baby son he _____ his opinion that the child would be extremely clever.
A declared B pronounced C spoke out
D expressed

10 Although she had been in prison for five years, she still had enough _____ to make jokes about her surroundings.
A courage B wit C interest D spirit

Group 10

1. This powerful nation is putting _____ on its weaker neighbour to give up some valuable land.
   A strength **B** influence **C** force **D** pressure

2. I must _____ to you that my delay in answering your letter is due mainly to laziness.
   A regret **B** apologise **C** confess **D** excuse

3. Your _____ for the post will be considered by the committee next week.
   A inquiry **B** claim **C** application **D** reference

4. _____ his retirement pension he has no income of any kind.
   A Beside **B** Apart from **C** In addition to
   D Let alone

5. The need for international action to prevent war between the two nations is _____.
   A urgent **B** immediate **C** instant **D** actual

6. The clerk was asked to _____ a number of mistakes in book-keeping he had made.
   A replace **B** settle **C** account for **D** control

7. He sat all day silently watching the fire and seemed to have no _____ at all left in him.
   A action **B** movement **C** life **D** mind

8. Scientists have carried out a great deal of _____ in the field of genetic engineering.
   A improvement **B** progress **C** invention
   D research

9. The colour of the dress was quite different under _____ light.
   A artificial **B** artistic **C** false **D** imitation

10. You have good reason not to trust him, but this time he is _____ trying to help you.
    A truthfully **B** faithfully **C** sincerely
    D honourably

Groups A–E are ungraded as in the examination

Group A

1. The library book is now overdue as I _____ have returned it a week ago.
   A must **B** could **C** should **D** had to

2. A small _____ is handy for minor electrical jobs in the home.
   A hammer **B** saw **C** screwdriver **D** file

3. Primitive man hunted and fought together with his own _____.
   A tribe **B** race **C** nation **D** society

4. _____ most of the furniture, it was clear that the roof and floors were also in a bad state of repair.
   A In case of **B** As well **C** Besides **D** Beside

5. A poet has to be extremely _____ to the music of words.
   A sensible **B** sentimental **C** alert **D** sensitive

6 The yearly procession to the temple in honour of the local god was an important religious _____ in that district.
   A custom   B feast   C habit   D activity

7 After such a long walk, his feet were so _____ that he could hardly get his shoes off.
   A padded   B tired   C stuffed   D swollen

8 With snow blocking all roads we had to make the journey in Morgan's _____.
   A van   B boat   C lorry   D truck

9 A feeling of tiredness almost _____ the soldier on duty and he had to struggle hard to keep awake.
   A overcame   B defeated   C conquered   D put out

10 You may have studied at university for five years but you are not _____ a highly-educated person.
    A finally   B certainly   C necessarily   D entirely

11 He could have gone straight there, but instead decided to follow the gently _____ river.
    A bending   B curling   C twisting   D winding

12 The room was so low that he had to bend his head to avoid the supporting _____.
    A bar   B beam   C block   D arch

13 Many people save money to _____ for their old age.
    A offer   B provide   C yield   D supply

14 My house is very _____ for getting to work as it is only a few minutes from the station.
    A useful   B fit   C convenient   D suitable

15 Those new dresses may be striking but that _____ does not suit everyone.
    A model   B form   C fashion   D sample

16 He _____ to climb the steep cliff but after only a few minutes decided it would be too dangerous.
    A dared   B risked   C practised   D attempted

17 The time taken on your journey, together with your _____, will enable you to calculate how far you have travelled.
    A rate   B speed   C motion   D distance

18 Nobody in this world is quite _____: we all have some faults.
    A right   B excellent   C perfect   D admirable

19 Thieves broke into the art gallery and _____ two of the paintings.
    A robbed   B burgled   C kidnapped   D stole

20 Town life offers a greater _____ of cinemas and restaurants.
    A chance   B amount   C difference   D variety

21 He had to _____ the mud off his shoes before coming into the house.
    A clear away   B kick   C scratch   D scrape

22 One of the _____ of country life is the difficulty of continuing one's education.
    A annoyances   B discomforts   C troubles   D drawbacks

23 You're surely not suggesting that these _____ young children could have planned such an evil thing.
    A lovely   B innocent   C natural   D pure

24 He _____ that he had ever been in prison.
    A denied   B disputed   C refused   D contradicted

25 One end of his single room was used as a kitchen but this was hidden behind a _____.
    A veil   B blind   C screen   D shield

Group B

1 Anyone who _____ in an examination is a thief as he is stealing marks that he has not earned.
   A cheats   B tricks   C takes in   D deceives

2 The class teacher punished disobedient pupils _____.
   A hardly   B severely   C strongly   D stiffly

3 Always ask for a _____ when you pay out money.
   A account   B cheque   C receipt   D record

4 Jim _____ Joe by calling him a thief but Joe only laughed at this.
   A insulted   B offended   C disgusted   D angered

5 When she cleaned the high windows, she always stood on a three-legged _____.
   A bench   B ladder   C stool   D chest

6 She earns money _____ small children while their parents are at work.
   A protecting   B minding   C helping   D caring

7 It was a great _____ to study under such an outstanding teacher.
   A privilege   B value   C favour   D fortune

8 Although he never claimed to be _____ he attended church every Sunday.
   A holy   B religious   C moral   D spiritual

9 It was a strange clock with an hour _____ that was longer than the minute one.
   A finger   B hand   C needle   D rod

10 You may never again have such an interesting _____ of travelling abroad.
    A advantage   B opportunity   C possibility   D occasion

11 _____ people always want more than they've got already.
    A Selfish   B Greedy   C Vain   D Jealous

12 William had sent his pen-friend a twenty-year-old photograph of himself and she nearly cried with _____ when they met.
   A disappointment   B despair   C astonishment   D deception

13 Although the car had stopped, the old lady _____ to step into the road in front of it.
   A postponed   B delayed   C paused   D hesitated

14 The bird was carrying a small branch in its _____.
   A beak   B feather   C paw   D teeth

15 On the 1st October a new government will be _____ by the nation for the next five years.
   A chosen   B elected   C voted   D proposed

16 He _____ the machine carefully to see why it had broken down.
   A examined   B controlled   C reviewed   D proved

17 People who distribute drugs like heroin can have no _____ at all.
   A goodness   B consciousness   C moral   D conscience

18 I haven't seen Joe _____: I wonder if he's ill.
   A lately   B previously   C beforehand   D earlier

19 Unless the transport strike ends soon, there will be a(n) _____ of food in the shops.
   A deficiency   B absence   C lack   D shortage

20 He _____ his toe into the pool and said the water was far too cold for swimming.
   A dug   B dipped   C dived   D sank

21 The dog lost interest when he realised the cat didn't intend to _____ away from him.
   A flee   B escape   C fly   D run

22 The curtains were made of a brightly-coloured _____ material woven locally.
   A coarse   B raw   C dark   D plastic

23 His main _____ in life is to gain money and power.
   A aim   B meaning   C determination   D decision

24 A last swing of the axe sent the old tree _____ to the ground.
   A bursting   B crashing   C rushing   D roaring

25 The table was a curious _____ as both the top and the legs were curved.
   A form   B pattern   C shape   D model

Group C

1 Would you please _____ again the meaning of the last sentence.
   A show   B explain   C describe   D inform

2 The icy _____ from under the door lowered the temperature in the room.
   A draught   B current   C drought   D gale

3 This beautiful desk has been owned by our family for a very long time and is probably now quite _____.
   A dear   B expensive   C precious   D valuable

4 I must buy a new leather _____ to go round my suitcase.
   A thread   B string   C rope   D strap

5 If I could _____ these shoes a little, they would be much more comfortable.
   A grow   B increase   C expand   D stretch

6 He was _____ to ten years' imprisonment.
   A judged   B sent   C convicted   D sentenced

7 Butter is covered with special paper so that no _____ can get through.
   A oil   B grease   C cream   D paste

8 The two lawyers _____ for a few minutes about the exact meaning of a point of law.
   A quarrelled   B discussed   C argued   D spoke up

9 In writing his account of these important events, he will not _____ his experiences in the order in which they happened.
   A classify   B compare   C compose   D arrange

10 He was wearing a navy blue tie over his cream _____.
   A shirt   B skirt   C jacket   D blouse

11 His parents, very poor but _____ people who never broke the law, were shocked when he was arrested for robbing a bank.
   A serious   B obedient   C respectable
   D responsible

12 Two men were _____ a large log over the rough ground with the help of a rope.
   A training   B drawing   C carrying   D dragging

13 The axe left lying on a bench in the rain was now covered with _____.
   A dirt   B mud   C dust   D rust

14 He usually telephones to say he is coming but this visit was a(n) _____ one.
   A unexpected   B extraordinary   C rare
   D unnoticed

15 A new interest in other countries and their problems is _____.
   A existing   B developing   C organising
   D advancing

16 Do you know the _____ for his sudden dislike of you?
   A origin   B cause   C effect   D reason

17 This coffee service is the only one of its kind so none of the cups and saucers can be _____.
   A copied   B substituted   C exchanged   D replaced

18 My tennis racket, fountain-pen and radio were all given to me by my aunt, who is a very _____ person.
   A generous   B sympathetic   C charitable
   D favourite

19 The towns are _____ by a good bus service.
    A combined   B connected   C joined   D united

20 He _____ the medicine quickly and then drank some orange juice.
    A swallowed   B spat   C licked   D sucked

21 He said he had _____ the performance of the new model and was surprised at what he had seen then.
    A judged   B worked out   C witnessed   D tried

22 The dog waiting behind the gate looked so _____ that I did not dare to go in.
    A wild   B harmful   C fierce   D bold

23 The hotel manager said he intended to _____ the less efficient members of his staff.
    A get rid of   B turn off   C give up   D resign

24 His ideas are sensible and logical but never in the least _____.
    A interested   B original   C intelligent   D clever

25 Playing games in the flower gardens is _____.
    A defended   B forbidden   C refused   D dismissed

Group D

1 Ten hours' unpaid overtime a week — you're little more than a _____!
   A fool   B slave   C servant   D beggar

2 By knocking down a bicycle standing at the roadside, he _____ his own car.
   A crushed   B destroyed   C damaged   D wrecked

3 Eight pounds for your room, three for dinner and two for lunch: the _____ cost will be thirteen pounds.
   A absolute   B entire   C whole   D total

4 The angry father _____ his son that he would turn him out of the house if he got into trouble once more.
   A scolded   B threatened   C blamed   D accused

5 There are almost _____ opportunities for a young person who wants to go off and find adventure.
   A continuous   B permanent   C universal
   D limitless

6 He got that _____ on his forehead when he ran into an open cupboard door in the dark a few days ago.
   A scar   B bruise   C blister   D sprain

7 You can buy almost anything in this shop; _____ it has a restaurant serving good cheap meals.
   A however   B meanwhile   C moreover
   D otherwise

8 He always asks how my family is whenever the two of us _____ in his office.
   A associate   B meet   C greet   D visit

9 She is a quite _____ woman, fairly pretty, fairly intelligent, but in no way special.
   A humble   **B** usual   **C** familiar   **D** ordinary

10 He works as a teacher but in this position cannot _____ enough to provide for his very large family.
   A earn   **B** gain   **C** win   **D** receive

11 Do you think there is any hope _____ of getting help?
   A anyhow   **B** indeed   **C** whatever   **D** probably

12 Although the examination he passed was not important, his success _____ him in his ambition to become a doctor.
   A persuaded   **B** urged   **C** convinced   **D** encouraged

13 He was a(n) _____ person who never smiled and who complained about everything.
   A miserable   **B** cross   **C** unfortunate   **D** sad

14 The Committee has approved your qualifications and you will be _____ to the retiring Head Clerk's post.
   A employed   **B** appointed   **C** admitted   **D** accepted

15 Immediately the writer realised his notes had disappeared, he searched the room he was in _____.
   A absolutely   **B** largely   **C** again   **D** thoroughly

16 I hope you don't _____ to my smoking.
   A disapprove   **B** object   **C** oppose   **D** disagree

17 When he lost his voice he could only _____ to his colleagues.
   A murmur   **B** stammer   **C** whisper   **D** whistle

18 The apple was so _____ that he put some sugar on it.
   A ripe   **B** sour   **C** bad   **D** juicy

19 Do you _____ how upset she was when you said you couldn't go to her party?
   A realise   **B** recognise   **C** observe   **D** feel

20 Newspapers get letters on many and _____ matters of interest.
   A different   **B** several   **C** various   **D** possible

21 The medicine he takes can only _____ the pain: it cannot get rid of it completely.
   A remedy   **B** heal   **C** solve   **D** relieve

22 The standard of our furniture is excellent but even so, we charge only _____ prices.
   A moderate   **B** small   **C** slight   **D** just

23 Every tooth in my upper _____ seemed to be aching.
   A chin   **B** cheek   **C** jaw   **D** throat

24 Nowadays builders must get _____ from the Planning Authorities before putting up new houses.
   A allowance   **B** permission   **C** liberty   **D** freedom

25 He was so _____ to his family that he could not bear to hear them criticised by anyone.
   A loyal   **B** affectionate   **C** true   **D** protective

Group E

1. It wouldn't do you any _____ to smoke less.
   A ill   B damage   C harm   D use

2. She always _____ a knot in her handkerchief to remind her of something she might forget.
   A fastens   B fixes   C ties   D does

3. We _____ not take our passports as we shan't be leaving the country.
   A may   B must   C ought   D need

4. Northern Europeans _____ to have fairer hair than people from further south.
   A incline   B tend   C use   D dispose

5. Your basic salary will be £15,000 and _____ you'll receive generous travel expenses.
   A otherwise   B in addition   C else   D in all

6. She works as an operator at the local telephone _____.
   A centre   B exchange   C office   D headquarters

7. I am _____ to have a quiet week-end.
   A hoping   B looking forward   C used   D wishing

8. A British doctor writes a _____ for medicine which a chemist or dispenser makes up.
   A prescription   B recipe   C receipt   D certificate

9. He's always asking if he can _____ my dictionary.
   A lend   B loan   C borrow   D hire

10. Do you think scientists will ever _____ all the mysteries of the universe?
    A resolve   B dissolve   C solve   D uncover

11. The trade negotiations in Brussels have unfortunately broken _____.
    A out   B down   C up   D off

12. The thousands who came to _____ the football match were disappointed when fog caused its cancellation.
    A view   B watch   C look at   D witness

13. Dr Sylvester will be making a _____ this evening.
    A talk   B speech   C lecture   D sermon

14. Will you help me to _____ for tomorrow's exam?
    A review   B read   C revise   D go through

15. I hesitate to consult a solicitor as I know his _____ will be high.
    A subscriptions   B fees   C costs   D contribution

16. Can you give me a(n) _____ as to how I can improve my English?
    A information   B advice   C help   D suggestion

17. The _____ age of the population of Ruritania is thirty-five.
    A average   B medium   C approximate   D normal

18. He is studying to become a member of the medical _____.
    A position   B profession   C employment   D post

19 He has turned _____ the offer of a job in Antarctica.
   A against **B** in **C** away **D** down

20 Her total _____, including the profits on her business, interest on investments and property rents, totalled £20,000.
   A salary **B** wage **C** income **D** earnings

21 After being friends for years, they _____.
   A fell off **B** fell out **C** fell over **D** fell through

22 My mother has presented me with three _____ of home-made jam.
   A jars **B** jugs **C** dishes **D** bowls

23 The loaf was covered with a golden-brown _____.
   A crust **B** shell **C** peel **D** coating

24 A newspaper _____ normally makes the final decision about the paper's contents.
   A publisher **B** reporter **C** editor **D** journalist

25 Good _____! I hope you do well.
   A hope **B** chance **C** wish **D** luck

Section B

In this section you will find after each of the passages a number of questions or unfinished statements about the passage, each with four suggested answers or ways of finishing it. You must choose the one which you think fits best. Write the number of each question or statement and after it the letters A, B, C and D. Then cross through the letter of the answer you choose. Give one answer only to each question. Read each passage right through before choosing your answers.

General advice

1 Read straight through the passage, noting carefully the different ideas introduced but above all getting a general idea of the contents.
2 Read through again much more slowly, examining in detail each statement made.
3 Do the same with the question items: a general read-through followed by detailed attention to each item.
4 Start matching each question item to the section of the passage it refers to, though remembering that in some cases the understanding of various parts of the passage may be involved in considering one question: a simple question may in fact refer to the passage as a whole.
5 The questions may require a clear understanding of vocabulary as part of meaning and may involve a rephrasing of an idea in different words. Often a single word in the passage may affect your choice.
    Intense concentration is needed to avoid the slightly false interpretations that may be suggested. If you are quite unsure, try cutting out what seem wrong answers and then examine the remaining possibilities.
6 Indicate your choice lightly in pencil so that you are still able to change your mind.
7 When you have completed all the questions you can, go through again for a second look at those left undone and for a second consideration of those already completed.

Note: Some candidates prefer to start the paper with Section B, indicating possible choices, before attempting Section A. After an interval, they often see new and more convincing possibilities when they return to Section B.

But remember to time the paper carefully — anything left unanswered will mean a loss of marks.

Group 1: Narrative

First passage

Luke Admont had disappeared. The old lady who cooked, cleaned and tidied for him called the police when he had not returned for two nights, explaining that he was seldom away from home and never without warning. According to her, he had no family and seemed to know hardly anybody in the neighbourhood. He spent his time studying and writing, though now and again he would work in the garden. Yet he was a pleasant gentleman, a little quiet perhaps, but always polite and although he had his likes and dislikes so far as food was concerned, he seldom interfered with the way she did her work.

One of the policemen interrupted her account by asking if they might perhaps see all the rooms in the house. Of course they were welcome to see whatever they wanted but apart from the hall where they now stood and Mr. Admont's sitting-room and bedroom, the house was quite bare, though indeed this did not apply to her own room and the kitchen and bathrooms. She suggested coming with them but her offer was refused politely as they could find their own way.

Two of the rooms above were indeed without furniture though the newly-polished floors suggested that the old lady did her duties well. Luke's bedroom provided little information about him. A bed, a large cupboard with two well-worn suits inside, a chest of drawers containing other clothes and a chair were all that could be seen. No pictures or photographs disturbed the neat striped pattern of the wallpaper.

The door of Luke's sitting-room, which was opposite the front door of the house, would not open. The younger policeman tried the handle, shook the door, looked through the keyhole and then called the old lady and asked if she had a key. The latter admitted that in fact, although she was forbidden to enter except when her employer was there, she had once left inside a brush she needed and had discovered a spare key on a shelf in the tool-shed, though this had been the only time she had used it. She produced it after some delay and the door swung open.

The two men paused, astonished, before they started to examine things in detail: the room was entirely different from the one they had inspected already. The walls were practically covered with books which, in addition, were heaped on both tables, all chairs except one which stood in front of an old-fashioned typewriter and even on the pale gold carpet. Whatever space remained was covered with sheets of paper, some unused in neat piles, others, overlaid with words, bundled together, impatiently it seemed. Elastic bands, envelopes, stamps and even a whole pack of playing cards, were scattered around the machine. Mrs. Seymour had clearly been telling the truth about Luke's interests.

1 The old lady was worried about Luke's disappearance largely because
   A he was always at home.
   B he never left home for more than one night.
   C he seldom went away without letting her know he was going.
   D he never went off without telling her.

2 The policeman asked about seeing the rooms in the house
   A politely.
   B impatiently.
   C sharply.
   D suspiciously.

3 From their inspection of the empty rooms the police
   A learned nothing at all.
   B got the impression that they might be used sometimes.
   C suspected that they were being prepared for someone.
   D noticed that they were being kept in good condition.

4 When asked about the key, the old lady
   A felt slightly guilty about having one.
   B told a lie about why she had one.
   C did not want to give the spare key to the police.
   D suddenly remembered that she did indeed have one.

5 What had Luke done with the papers he had typed?
   A He had scattered them about the floor.
   B He had arranged them in piles.
   C He had gathered them together untidily.
   D He had left them lying round the typewriter.

Second passage

Mr. and Mrs. Barber had been having one of their more bitter quarrels, or at least, Mr. Barber had been quarrelling with his wife. This happened regularly once a month and the argument usually ended with Mrs Barber's apologising and promising to be more careful and with Mr. Barber's sigh-
5 ing impatiently, picking up his walking-stick and going out to his club. This time however Mrs. Barber had not apologised but had seized her umbrella — it was the wettest night for the past two years — and disappeared, saying that she might or might not come back; she was going to her club, a statement that surprised her husband as he had never known
10 she had one.
   The trouble had started as usual over money, or rather, the recording of money in the immense black account-book in which Mr. Barber insisted that every cash payment, for food, clothes, the window-cleaner, the milkman, stamps, bus fares and the church collection, all must be written
15 down, dated and added up every two days, the total to be compared with the remaining money in Mrs. Barber's handbag. As a clerk in a supermarket company, Mr. Barber earned his living recording money spent and profits gained in even more immense account-books and absolutely delighted in doing it. Mrs. Barber found it a nuisance. She could almost
20 smell where the best bargains were and she managed to run her home extremely efficiently on her husband's rather miserable salary. But when she returned from shopping, she had to prepare dinner and wash up, and by then she had forgotten exactly how she had spent every penny and she hated cheating.

Once a month her husband examined the account-book and bitter accusations followed. Mrs. Barber, who was a gentle, sweet person, would admit her guilt and, during the next four weeks, would try to remember to write down everything, even the right date.

But a week later she was already puzzling over how exactly she had spent that five-pound note and at the end of two weeks, the gaps in her record were only too clear.

On this occasion, however, Mrs. Barber refused to accept her husband's criticism. For only the day before a friend had called with a briefcase containing twenty five-pound notes and Mr. Barber's passport and driving licence. 'I found this in a telephone-box,' he said. 'It must be your husband's.' Mrs. Barber put it away carefully. That evening her husband came home late when his wife was already asleep and he left in a hurry the next morning, saying nothing about his loss. But on his return at six in the evening, he immediately called for the account-book and as usual started to complain and scold. 'As you are so careless,' he said, 'you must learn your lesson. I see from here you have spent less than half the money I gave you. The other half can last you for this month. You don't need any more now.'

It was at this point that Mrs. Barber seized her umbrella and walked out.

1 Why was Mr. Barber astonished?
   A He was astonished about where she was going.
   B He had not expected his wife to behave in this way.
   C He was the one who normally spent the evening in his club.
   D He could not imagine why his wife was so angry.

2 Mr. Barber was impatient with his wife because
   A she was not a good housekeeper.
   B she was not what he considered to be careful.
   C she wasted his money.
   D she was unwilling to do what he asked her.

3 How did Mrs. Barber regard her husband's commands?
   A They very much annoyed her.
   B They seemed a good idea but a difficult one to carry out.
   C She wanted to obey him but found it impossible.
   D She was unwilling to take the trouble.

4 Why didn't Mrs. Barber avoid trouble by writing down false figures?
   A She was afraid her husband would find this out.
   B She was an honest person.
   C She was not clever enough to do this.
   D It was too difficult to do this.

5 Why did Mrs. Barber walk out?
   A She knew she could not manage without any more money.
   B She was angry about her husband's dishonesty.
   C She was angry because he wanted to punish her.
   D She could live on the money the friend had brought.

Third passage

Only the probably comparatively rare single person who has changed lodgings frequently, bearing most of his property from one furnished flat to another in some distant place, has truly experienced the entirely different feelings that are connected with leaving and arriving, with packing to go and unpacking to stay.

Unless one hates the place one is leaving, packing to go is nothing but a worrying, tiring, thoroughly unpleasant experience. There is never, on any occasion, enough time. The whole operation is at first wisely and efficiently planned, with careful attention to detail. Several days in advance the first steps are taken. Old letters are read again and many are laid aside for destruction. Photographs which have long remained unsorted are examined and then usually stuffed back into their envelopes for a further inspection and arrangement when time allows. Letters with the new address are written to friends. Then comes the sudden shock: moving-day is only forty-eight hours ahead. An odd collection of trunks, suitcases and bags soon covers the floor and all the now extraordinary confusion of clothes, books, letters and postcards, cushions, shoes, records, pots, pans and plates, unopened tins of food, twice as many objects, it seems, as can ever be fitted into anything, slowly disappears into the ever-decreasing space. At any moment some other half-forgotten duty demands attention: clothes to be collected from the cleaner's, bills to be paid, visits to the bank, borrowed books to be returned; besides the problem of cooking meals from the left-over food and eating them in no time at all. No sleep the last night, with the moment when all must be standing ready closed and waiting pressing unhesitatingly nearer and with floors to sweep, carpets to brush, a kitchen to wash: everything to be left in perfect order. The astonishing thing is that in some extraordinary way, everything is — just — ready and the rooms are left reasonably clean and tidy.

But how really enjoyable is the unpacking to stay that follows! For there is now limitless time in which to make a new and delightful home. These shelves for books, arranged in a suitable order; these cupboards for clothes, for papers, handwork, notepaper, the (still undestroyed) letters from friends. A pause, while one goes out to explore the neighbourhood, the new interesting surroundings, and then, surprisingly quickly, all the arranging has been completed and one can sit back contentedly with a cup of coffee, at ease in a new home that is just different enough to be exciting and just as much the same as to be pleasantly familiar.

1 What is the main idea being developed in this passage?
   A The anxiety and difficulties experienced when moving to another home.
   B A comparison between the experiences of preparation for moving and of settling into a new home.
   C Some of the less pleasant sides of moving from place to place.
   D A comparison of the feelings a person has towards an old home and a new one.

2 What happens to the photographs?
   A They are sorted out ready to be arranged later.
   B They remain untouched.
   C It is decided what will happen to them at some other time.
   D Some attention is given to them.

3   How does the person packing manage to be ready in time?
    A   He organises the available time efficiently.
    B   He works all through the nights.
    C   This is difficult to explain.
    D   He gives every moment to his packing, not even stopping to prepare food.

4   The most important difference between packing and unpacking is that
    A   there isn't the same need to hurry when unpacking.
    B   there is much more space in the new home.
    C   it takes less time to unpack than to pack.
    D   there is no need to clean and tidy the new home.

5   What special charm has the new home when it is ready?
    A   It combines the interest of the new with the enjoyment of the known.
    B   All around there are new things to discover.
    C   Everything is the same but in new surroundings.
    D   The person moving can take his own world with him.

Fourth passage

I admit I am a complete fool about cats, who, for some reason I don't understand, fail to return my admiration. I will wait minutes for cars to pass so that I can cross the road to address a black and white cat at ease in sunshine on a low wall, either to watch the tip of a frightened tail disappear
5   under a neighbouring gate or to be met with the most violent cat curses or, while my hand moves gently over the smooth shining fur, to be bitten or scratched or attacked in both ways at the same time. It makes no difference: I continue my journey with my respect increased. After all, the wisest men of one of the oldest civilisations worshipped the noble cat so why
10 should I be ashamed of following their example?
    I have sometimes stayed long enough in one place to be owned by a cat and it is on those occasions that I at last feel sympathy with parents who cannot control their children. I have the firmest belief in discipline, especially for the cat who adopts me and is kind enough to allow me to
15 share her home and provide her with food. She will have a comfortable basket and not sit on any furniture; she will come when called or have no supper; and she will at all times behave towards me with the respect I show towards her. And then what happens? She refuses even to consider the basket, and, as soon as my back is turned, settles on my favourite chair,
20 daring me to move her on my return. At some unexpected moment after I have sat down, she springs suddenly on to my knees and delightedly ruins my stockings with her claws, complaining angrily, even painfully with the sharpest of teeth, if I bend down to pick something up. I dare not rise to change the television programme, however much I dislike it, and she
25 watches dreamily the moving shadows on the screen. She comes not to my call, but when she is ready, hours later, and I am so relieved to see her that her supper is increased in amount. When put out at night (with fierce disapproval) she waits till I am asleep and then cries noisily at my bedroom window to come in. An hour later she cries even more noisily at the bed-
30 room door to be let out again.
    If I go away on holiday, a neighbour feeds her, who reports on my return on her sweetness, her obedience and perfect behaviour. I am the only one that she delights in defying.

Dogs are pleasant animals, friendly, faithful and intelligent. Dogs have a proper respect for the human race. You know where you are with a dog; never with a cat, who will be selfish, vain, ungrateful and quite unreasonable. But that's just it. Who wants to know where he is with any living thing? It is the free, the strange creature of grace and beauty, the independent and unknown, that attracts, not the worthy, respectful, dependable slave.

1 What are the writer's feelings for cats?
   A She gives them unreturned worship.
   B They are a combination of annoyance and intense admiration.
   C She is quite fond of them.
   D She is ashamed of being their slave.

2 What conditions does the writer make when she gives a cat a home?
   A She expects the cat to obey her.
   B The cat must observe a few necessary rules.
   C The cat must accept the writer's authority.
   D The cat will stay only if she behaves herself.

3 One example of the cat's refusal to do as she is told is
   A her dislike of her basket.
   B her destruction of the writer's clothes.
   C her attacks on the writer when the latter tries to move.
   D her settling comfortably on furniture.

4 What happens about the cat's evening meal?
   A She gets more food because she is more hungry when she comes home late.
   B She gets less food because she has not answered the writer's call.
   C She gets more food for having come home.
   D She gets extra food because the writer can stop worrying.

5 What happens before the writer goes to bed?
   A The cat is carried out complaining bitterly.
   B She walks out intensely angry.
   C She keeps trying to come straight in again.
   D Once outside she starts making a noise so that she is readmitted.

Fifth passage

And now came the problem of getting out. On either side of Richard stretched a row of listeners, their eyes half-closed as they followed the complicated pattern of the music: most respectable, well-dressed, well-fed ladies and gentlemen, who would not be pleased if they were forced to stand up to let him pass, walking on their feet, knocking against them. But the train would be leaving in twenty minutes and it was the last one so he must risk unpopularity. There were fewer seats to the right so he whispered 'Excuse me' to his neighbour, who was clearly rudely shocked out of a pleasant dream but unwillingly raised himself and pressed against the back of his seat while Richard moved past. The sudden stir warned those beyond, who equally unwillingly flattened themselves, while he cautiously lowered his feet on to firm ground. His programme slipped to the floor and there was some confusion as heads almost knocked in an effort to find it, but Richard was too ashamed to stop for it. One figure remained before

15 the freedom of the space between the seat rows: a large, baby-faced, white-haired old man who was clearly fast asleep. With an immense effort Richard stepped over his knees, and, conscious of angry looks from all sides, crept down the passage to the doors.

Now he must find his hat, coat and scarf. In a room reached by a large 20 hole in the wall, hundreds of coats hung from hooks, each with a number on it. He retrieved his ticket from his pocket. But there was nobody to take it, as the women responsible had hurried off for a quick cup of tea before the rush began. Indeed, there was nobody at all in sight. Richard did the only thing possible: he climbed through into the room. He was relieved to 25 find his things at the end of a row, but, just as he was climbing back, a voice said angrily, 'Just a minute, sir. What do you think you are doing?' Two men, clearly members of the theatre staff, were waiting for him threateningly. Richard hesitated, with his hat and scarf held in front of him, almost, he felt, as if they were some kind of protection, and possibly 30 something of the guilt he had felt at disturbing the concert-goers still on his face. Then he held out his ticket and pointed to the one on his collar. 'I'm sorry. I've got to catch a train,' he said unpinning the ticket as he spoke, and putting one arm into the coat. The taller man compared the tickets suspiciously, and disapprovingly stepped aside, while Richard drew on the 35 other sleeve, pulled the gloves from the pocket and hurried through the door into the street.

1 Most of the people around Richard were
   A listening intently.
   B half asleep.
   C unaware of anything that was happening.
   D studying their copies of the music being played.

2 He decided to move towards the right because
   A he would be nearer the way out.
   B there would be more space to move in.
   C there were several empty seats.
   D he would have less distance to go to get to the end of the row.

3 When Richard left his seat we know he was carrying
   A his programme and the ticket for his coat.
   B his programme and his entrance ticket.
   C his gloves and his programme.
   D his programme.

4 How did Richard feel when the two men stopped him?
   A unnecessarily alarmed.
   B rightly impatient.
   C thoroughly innocent.
   D somewhat annoyed.

5 Where was the ticket on Richard's coat?
   A sticking out of the pocket.
   B tied to the belt.
   C fastened to the top of the coat.
   D pinned to the front of the coat.

Group 2: Informative

First passage

The idea of working 'au pair', with full board and pocket money in return for help in the home, has been welcomed by thousands of girls coming from countries outside Britain. Many of them want to practise the English they have learned at school but cannot afford to live away from home without some kind of work to provide them with at least the necessities of life.

The aim of practising the language may be weaker in some girls than the desire to enjoy the freedom of being away from home and the excitement of living in a large city like London. The idea of working seriously for their living may be unattractive. It is experiences with the kind of girl who returns home at all hours of the night or not at all, is always complaining when asked to do anything, cannot be trusted to do the simplest thing properly, neglects her studies and gets into various kinds of trouble, that make many employers hesitate about taking a second 'au pair' into their home.

But the faults are not all on one side and many 'au pair' girls also have good cause for complaint, some of them becoming depressed and unhappy as a result. Unfortunately far too few girls who are attracted by the idea of earning their living in another land are prepared for the various difficulties that may await them.

It is essential that any girl who takes a post of this kind should be at least eighteen years old, and be sensible, practical and well able to look after herself. Wherever possible she should go to a family she knows something about, possibly from a friend who has already worked with them. In any case she should make sure she has from her employer a letter stating clearly her terms of employment: exactly what she is expected to do (whether minding children or helping with light housework), how long she will be expected to work each week and her free days and half-days for attending language classes. She should be promised a single room of a satisfactory standard and she will want to eat with the family to have the opportunity of practising the language with them. Her earnings will not be high, but she must know exactly what they will be and when they will be paid. Her employer will probably pay her return travel expenses, if the girl is prepared to stay with the same family all the time.

Two other pieces of advice are important. A girl should keep with her travellers' cheques of a sufficient value to pay for her journey home in case it becomes necessary to return urgently. In addition she should know the addresses of one or two organisations which can give help and advice if there are problems. Several of these organisations exist in London and other large centres.

1 What can an au pair girl expect from her employers?
   A   Somewhere to stay, meals and some money.
   B   Everything she will need including money.
   C   A fully-furnished room and some money.
   D   A salary, room and food.

2 Which of the following do some employers complain about in their au-pair girls?
   A   Inability and lack of interest in their job.
   B   Dishonesty.
   C   Leaving without warning.
   D   Dissatisfaction with pay and conditions.

3   One of the qualities that an intending au pair should possess is
    A   a desire to work really hard.
    B   the ability to face unexpected difficulties.
    C   an interest in new experiences.
    D   the ability to do housework or take care of children.

4   An intending au pair girl should make sure she has a letter from her employer which states
    A   her duties.
    B   local opportunities for studying English.
    C   opportunities for conversation with the family.
    D   her daily hours of work.

5   Why should an au pair girl have travellers' cheques available?
    A   In case she wants to give up her post.
    B   To meet any unexpected difficulty.
    C   To provide for her return home in case of need.
    D   To have some form of money that cannot be stolen.

Second passage

The seller or his agents are not obliged in law to tell you of the defects or true condition of the house. So it is important that your own surveyor is sent to make a structural survey of the house after you have made an offer for it, but before you enter into legal commitment.

5   Your surveyor's job is to find out all the internal and exterior defects in the house and to indicate to you how much money it will cost to put them right. He will tell you whether the house is worth the price being asked, and may suggest a price to negotiate with the seller. If he does his job well, he will earn his fee (which for a straightforward survey of a five-room house
10 is not likely to be less than £50) by providing information which can be used to start negotiations.

Many defects are not apparent to the ordinary house buyer but can be detected by the expert — the surveyor. The building society or local authority from which you hope to get a loan will send its surveyor too,
15 whose fee you will have to pay. This surveyor makes only a valuation (not a full survey) to see whether the property is good security for the part of the purchase price you might be lent. His report is confidential and may not be available to you, though building societies may be prepared to tell the purchaser about really major defects following their valuation. They may
20 in fact make it a condition of the mortgage that you will have the defects repaired within a stated time (at your own expense of course).

If you are buying a new house, you will also need assurance that the house is properly built and that the builder will accept responsibility for any defects that may appear due to poor design, materials or workman-
25 ship. If a builder is registered with the National House-Builders' Registration Council you will know that the house has been spot-check inspected at periodic intervals during building. Arbitration machinery, and, for newly-built houses, a 10-year protection against major structural defects, exist should things go wrong and the builder seek to avoid responsibility.

30 If the builder is not registered it will be wise to get a competent surveyor to check the house over during various stages of construction. (He will charge a fee for each visit to the site.)

Note: a mortgage is money lent by a bank or other organisation to a house-buyer, with the house as security for repayment.

1   At what stage in buying a house is a surveyor employed?
    A   After you have inspected the house yourself.
    B   Shortly before you take up residence in the house.
    C   Before you have any kind of discussion about the price.
    D   During the early stage of free negotiations.

2   What is the main reason for employing a surveyor?
    A   To inspect and report on the condition of the house.
    B   To tell you the true value of the house.
    C   To assist you in negotiating for a lower price.
    D   To advise you about carrying out repairs.

3   Why does the building society or local authority send its own surveyor?
    A   To provide them with the information they need in advising the possible buyer.
    B   To check the report prepared by the buyer's surveyor.
    C   To check what repairs the buyer must carry out before getting a loan.
    D   To find out whether it will be advisable to lend the purchase money.

4   The main difference between the surveyors employed by you and the building society is that
    A   the second surveyor is not interested in the defects of the house.
    B   you do not have to pay the second surveyor.
    C   the second surveyor's job is to decide what the house is worth.
    D   the second surveyor's job is to find out whether the house is fit to live in.

5   The buyer of a new house has to be sure that
    A   the construction of the house has been constantly supervised.
    B   serious constructional faults will be put right during a certain period.
    C   he will have legal protection in the case of a dispute with the builder.
    D   the builder is registered with the National Housebuilders' Registration Council.

Third passage

Do I really want to go on to higher education?
   This is the first question you must ask yourself and it is the most important at this major crossroads of your life. Many can advise you, but you alone face the consequences of this fundamental decision.
5   Stop. Think about it. Be honest with yourself and be realistic. Do you want higher education because you really feel you will benefit from it — or are you drifting towards it in response to the expectations of your parents and friends? Conversely, are you being put off higher education by other people's prejudices?
10   Don't commit yourself to any form of full-time higher education if you are not interested in any of the numerous courses available. Higher education is most uncomfortable and unsatisfying for those who have little interest in the subject they have chosen to study.
   It can be an advantage to have a clear idea about the kind of career you
15   eventually want, because then you can choose a course most likely to equip you for your future.

Don't worry if you have no ideas about a future career; but do find out what are the career implications of your choice of course. Broad prospects will be open to you whatever course you follow, provided you do well and have the right personal qualities. Don't typecast yourself — or allow anyone else to do so. This particularly applies to girls. Girls are still subject to prejudices about courses which lead to careers traditionally labelled as 'man's work'. This is almost always unjustifiable and women are now working in all sorts of former male 'preserves'.

Competition for places will be tougher in future but the total available will still be very large.

Seek advice from your careers teacher, careers officer and parents — but it is you who must decide whether or not you want to go on to higher education.

1. Your attitude towards going on to higher education is most important because
   - A this is the moment in your life when you have to decide your future.
   - B it is a time when you can get plenty of advice.
   - C you will be the one affected by any decision you make.
   - D the wrong attitude is likely to have very serious consequences.

2. A decision to continue studying should depend on
   - A the advantages you believe you will have from doing so.
   - B advice from experienced people.
   - C the career you are hoping to take up.
   - D family considerations.

3. Your choice of study subjects should depend on
   - A the extent to which they will be useful to you.
   - B your own feelings about them.
   - C their value to you in your future career.
   - D your ability in these subjects.

4. What advice is given about your future career plans?
   - A These must be definite before deciding on study subjects.
   - B They should not influence your choice of study subjects.
   - C You should be aware of the career prospects of the course you take.
   - D Any course can prepare you for a suitable career.

5. If you 'typecast' yourself you
   - A study only the subjects you are good at.
   - B are influenced by your own personal interests.
   - C are prepared to adopt any course of study.
   - D accept other people's views about what you should study.

Group 3: Public notices, instructions, advertisements etc.

First passage

Thousands of jobs come into our Jobcentres and Employment offices every week, but they get snapped up quickly. So although we shall do all we can to help you, it's important for you to do all you can to help yourself.

This leaflet tells you how.

Registered for work

Once you have registered for work we will match you against available vacancies. You must also register for work at the Jobcentre in order to claim unemployment benefit. But you actually apply for benefit at the local unemployment office.

Getting a job through self-service

Jobs that come in are put on self-service display as soon as possible. Half the people who find jobs through Jobcentres or Employment offices find them through self-service. You can call in at any time to look at the jobs displayed.

The receptionist is here to help you, so if you see a job that looks right for you, tell the receptionist, giving the reference number on the card.

If you want further help with finding a job

If you want more help or advice, don't forget that's what we're here for. Our Employment Advisers can help you with things like:
- thinking about the different sorts of jobs you could do — and which are best for you
- jobs available locally or elsewhere
- training for a new job
- your suitability for a TOPS training course, with a tax-free allowance
- grants to help you look for, and move to, work in other parts

Even though you have a clear idea of the sort of job and pay you want, you may find that something different will suit you quite well. Keep this in mind when you're talking with the Employment Adviser.

If you don't find a job on your first visit

Pop into self-service as often as you can to look at the jobs on display there.

Good vacancies are coming in all the time but they do go quickly.

Don't rely on being told about them just because you've been registered for employment.

If you can't get to the office easily, come in whenever you can — and enquire by telephone as often as you like.

It'll help you to find a job faster if you keep in touch.

1. The purpose of this leaflet is to
   A. provide general advice about what to do when you haven't a job.
   B. suggest how to get maximum benefit from a certain employment service.
   C. give information about services available for unemployed people.
   D. help to reduce the number of unemployed people.

2. The people most likely to get jobs are those who
   A. make use of job-information services at the Jobcentre as often as possible.
   B. regularly ask for help and advice at the Jobcentre.
   C. use their own ideas and commonsense in looking for a job.
   D. register for work immediately the need arises.

3. Unemployed people can claim benefits from the unemployment office only if they
   A. first inform the Jobcentre that they have lost their job.
   B. register at the local unemployment office.
   C. claim the benefits both at the Jobcentre and the unemployment office.
   D. first inform the Jobcentre of their availability for work.

4. The TOPS course allowance is
   A. cost-of-living expenses while on the course.
   B. permission to attend the course.
   C. a salary for work done on the course.
   D. an additional payment for qualifications gained on the course.

5. It is suggested that if you really want a job you will be willing to
   A. be reasonably adaptable in your requirements.
   B. take any job you are able to do.
   C. apply for a large variety of jobs.
   D. take a suitable job elsewhere.

Top tips for good riders

Concentration is the keystone of good riding

Complete concentration will enable you to see and to take NOTICE of every significant detail.

Small details noted are clues to possible hazards.

Small details missed lead to accidents and near misses.

Concentration helps skilful handling of your machine, the avoidance of bad gear changes, late and fierce braking and the skids which almost inevitably follow the locking of the wheels through fierce braking on bad surfaces.

Concentration assists anticipation

Think before acting

A good driver may appear, to the less experienced, to be riding automatically, but the truth is that through concentration and anticipation, he has developed the art of riding.

Every corner or bend, every gear change or manoeuvre, creates a problem which can only be solved by thinking.

The thoughtful rider always has time in hand, time to decide whether it is best to accelerate out of danger or to avoid it by stopping.

Think — anticipate — and avoid accidents

Use speed intelligently and keep it in its place.

It is not always safe to go as fast as 30 m.p.h. in built-up areas; in some circumstances it would be highly dangerous to do so but, where circumstances permit, riding at an even speed in conformity with the traffic stream assists in maintaining an orderly traffic flow.

High speeds are safe only when there is a clear view of the road ahead for a considerable distance. In fact speed should be governed by
(a) the distance seen to be clear
(b) the conditions of weather and road surface
(c) traffic density
(d) speed limits in force

At 60 m.p.h. a motor-cycle travels a distance of 88 feet per second. A second or more could easily pass between seeing an emergency and applying the brakes.

Any fool can ride fast enough to be dangerous.

1. The concentration referred to in the first sentence refers mainly to
    A   hard thinking about handling your machine.
    B   an awareness of circumstances that suggest possible trouble.
    C   constant calculation of the speed of your machine in relation to other traffic.
    D   an ability to brake immediately in case of emergency.

2. If the good driver were really 'riding automatically' he would be
    A   making valuable use of his experience when riding.
    B   riding satisfactorily without active thought or planning.
    C   dealing intelligently with all the problems of riding in traffic.
    D   handling all situations with concentration.

3. A characteristic of a thoughtful driver is that he
    A   has developed a safe technique for overtaking other vehicles.
    B   reacts immediately in deciding on the safest course.
    C   knows exactly what to do in a possibly dangerous situation.
    D   avoids the necessity for an instantaneous reaction in an emergency.

4. In the advice about using speed intelligently, motor cyclists are advised to
    A   adapt their own speed to that of other vehicles.
    B   ride always at a moderate speed.
    C   avoid unnecessary changes in speed.
    D   regard speed limits in towns as a maximum not a minimum.

5. When is it always unsafe to ride fast?
    A   When the rider cannot see a long way in front of him.
    B   When there is other traffic ahead.
    C   When the rider is exceeding the speed limit.
    D   When it is impossible to stop unexpectedly.

THE LADY JANE HOTEL

The management and staff are happy to welcome you and will do all they can to make your stay an enjoyable one.
We hope you will find the following suggestions and information of use to you.

MEAL TIMES
Our overnight charge includes a continental-type breakfast.

Breakfast	7.30–9.30 a.m.
Lunch	12.00–2.00 p.m.
Afternoon tea	4.00–5.30 p.m.
Dinner	7.00–9.15 p.m.

Meals can be served in rooms at a small extra charge. We regret that owing to staff arrangements, meals cannot be served outside these times. In exceptional circumstances please consult one of our receptionists in advance.

Light refreshments, including tea, coffee, biscuits and sandwiches, can be served in rooms between 10 a.m. to 11 p.m. except during the meal times listed above. Cold drinks are available in the room refrigerator.

ROOM CLEANING
Please hang the appropriate sign on your door handle if you do not wish to be disturbed. It will facilitate the duties of the chambermaids however if the room can be vacated temporarily at any time between 9 a.m. and 4 p.m.

VALUABLES
The hotel cannot be responsible for the loss of money, jewellery or other valuables unless they are deposited in the hotel safe and signed for by the manager or his deputy.

DEPARTURES
Please inform reception of your intended departure before 9.30 a.m. of the day concerned. Rooms must be vacated by noon to allow for their preparation for incoming guests. We regret that their retention after that time will necessitate a further night's charge. If circumstances require, luggage can be left temporarily in the charge of the Hall Porter.

A SPECIAL REQUEST
We would respectfully suggest that in consideration of the comfort of other guests the volume of radios and televisions should be moderated after 11 p.m.

While the management and staff would like to think that our service and arrangements are of a standard that will ensure your complete satisfaction, we should warmly welcome suggestions for improvement. If you should find anything that is not up to standard, please inform reception who will take immediate steps to put matters right.

1 The general purpose of this notice is to provide guests with
   A a summary of the daily routine of the hotel.
   B instructions about how to behave in the hotel.
   C facts about the running of the hotel.
   D information they may need during their stay.

2 The general tone of the notice is
   A cold and officious.
   B firm but courteous.
   C sensible but with little concern for the guests.
   D informative but insincere.

3 Dinner could be served at half past nine
   A under no circumstances.
   B easily by prior arrangement.
   C if such a request were considered justified.
   D only in the guest's own room at extra charge.

4 At what time can light refreshments be served in rooms?
   A 9.45 a.m.
   B 1.45 p.m.
   C 3.45 p.m.
   D 11.45 p.m.

5 The sign that can be hung on the door handle
   A requests the postponement of room cleaning.
   B indicates the time when the room can be cleaned.
   C shows that the guest does not want the room to be cleaned that day.
   D informs the maid that the room is now ready for cleaning.

6 After 11 p.m. guests are
   A instructed to make less noise.
   B required to turn off their radios and TVs.
   C requested not to disturb other guests by causing too much unnecessary noise.
   D reminded that any kind of noise in their rooms can disturb others.

Paper 2 Composition

Introduction

The following composition subjects have been arranged in groups, each of which represents one of the different types of composition which may appear on the examination paper.

When practising the writing of compositions, pay careful attention to these points:

1. Instructions are always given about the number of words to be used. You are likely to lose marks if you fail to follow these instructions.

2. Two compositions are required out of the five suggested. Choose carefully those two subjects about which you have the ability and language command to write well. (See 5 below)

3. One and a half hours are allowed for this paper. The consideration, preparation and writing of each composition should be completed in 35–40 minutes, allowing at least 5 minutes for reading through.

4. Read through the subject as it is expressed on the paper very carefully and *make sure you are writing on this subject* and not on what, after a hurried reading, you think is the one wanted. Marks are lost by failure to write on the subject given.

5. Gather some ideas. Do not be too ambitious. It is dangerous to try to express ideas which you have not the vocabulary or general command of English to deal with correctly — however interesting they may be.

6. Arrange the ideas you have gathered, grouping them in paragraphs. A composition of about 150 words will probably include three paragraphs, though in some cases two or four are possible.

7. *Think in English and do not translate from your own language*. Use only the English sentences and expressions which you know to be correct, even though these may not allow you to express your ideas so well as you could do in your own language. Ideas that have been translated very seldom sound natural in another language, even when translated correctly, and translation encourages mistakes.

8. When you have finished, *read your work through very carefully and critically* so that you can find at least some of the mistakes before the examiner does.

9. Assessment of marks: The mark is based on a general impression of
    (a) vocabulary range and suitability
    (b) sentence structure range and suitability
    (c) grammar, punctuation, spelling
    (d) subject matter as related to the question
    (e) planning and organisation

Subjects for composition

Choose one or more of the subjects to write about for each type of composition. Your answers should follow the instructions given exactly, and be of between 120 and 180 words each. Not more than 45 minutes should be spent on any composition, including at least 5 minutes for reading through.

Letter-writing

General advice

The beginning, dating and ending of each of these letters should be like those of an ordinary English letter, but should not be counted in the number of words used.

The way in which the ideas are expressed will depend on the kind of person who will be receiving the letter.

In many cases your letter will seem more natural if you include some short greetings and remarks in addition to what you write on the given subject.

Suggestion for a letter

You are doing a holiday job, either in a kindergarten for children between three and five years old or as an assistant in a sports holiday centre for schoolchildren between eleven and fourteen. Write a letter to a friend who is thinking of doing the same job, giving a short account of a typical day's work.

Advice: This letter would be a long one if a detailed description were given. Selection and compression (saying a lot in a few words) are important here.

Plan: 1 Reason for writing.
2 Length of the working day.
3 How it is spent.
4 Short final comment.

> 25 Green Avenue
> Mapleham MH2 HM3
> Northshire
> 28th February, 19--

Dear Susan,

Jane has told me you are interested in kindergarten work and would like to know something about the job I'm doing so I'll try to describe a typical day.

Our children spend both morning and afternoon here as their mothers have full-time jobs, so we're with them from eight o'clock till half past four. Hot meals are delivered but we supervise lunch.

Part of the morning is spent out of doors whenever possible, playing in the garden or the park or going for a walk. Indoors we play with the toys and other equipment available, join in singing and other games or activities, making pictures, modelling and constructing, and sometimes we all watch and talk about short video films. The children sleep for an hour after lunch and then play indoors or out until their mothers arrive.

Yes, it's tiring work but immensely enjoyable and I'm sure you wouldn't regret taking it on.

Yours sincerely,

Mary Smith (153 words)

Notes:
1. Your address only (*not* your name) must appear in the top right-hand corner.
2. The date comes under your address.
3. A letter beginning 'Dear Susan/Mr James' ends 'Yours sincerely'.
   A letter beginning 'Dear Sir/Madam' ends 'Yours faithfully'.
4. In the case of a business or formal letter, the name and address of the person receiving the letter stands below the date but on the left hand side of the page.

Subjects

1. A friend who will soon be visiting your town has written to ask whether he/she may stay in your home during the visit. Though your friend would usually be welcome, for some reason you cannot give an invitation this time. Write to the friend, apologising for and explaining this, suggesting some other possible arrangement and expressing the hope that you can meet and entertain your friend during the visit.
2. An intelligent young relative or friend, who had planned to study for a profession, suddenly writes to say that at sixteen he/she is tired of school, and intends to leave and find a job, so as to earn money and be independent. You believe that later the boy or girl will very much regret this decision. Write your reply to the letter you have received.
3. You hear that a very old and beautiful building in your town is to be destroyed in order to make room for a petrol station. Write a letter to a local newspaper explaining why you think something should be done to save the building.
4. You have read a book written by an English person which you admire but which in one or two ways gives a false idea of your country. In a letter to the writer of the book, say how much you enjoyed it but also point out the ideas you consider to be untrue.
5. You keep in touch with a former schoolfriend by enclosing a letter with the annual Christmas card. Write the letter you might send at the end of a year in which nothing specially important has happened.

Description

General advice

Most short descriptions can concern only facts, the choosing of essential details and their intelligent arrangement. The more imaginative type of description would demand a higher standard of expression than is expected at First Certificate level.

Some subjects suggest their own arrangement (see 3 below). Others however (the description of a picture for example) need a good deal of thought in planning.

Here is a suggested plan for the first of the subjects.

Plan:
1. The main subject of the picture.
2. The surroundings and/or other details.
3. The qualities you admire in it.

Expression should be clear and simple without any attempt at 'fine' writing. It is best to avoid spoken forms in writing, including verbal abbreviations and other conversational forms.

Subjects

1. Describe a picture you admire very much.
2. Describe someone who is completely different from anyone else you know.

3 Describe an attractive camping-ground, referring also to its surroundings and some of the services provided.
4 You have a room which has a particularly ugly view. Describe what you can see.
5 You are almost certain that some examination results are going to arrive soon after breakfast on a certain morning. Describe your feelings while you are waiting for the postman, at the moment of opening the very important letter and after you have read the contents.

Narrative

General advice

The limited number of words you can use makes it necessary to give a general idea of only one or two happenings: there can be a very few descriptive details but your main concern should be the story itself.

Sometimes you are given the main lines of the story and you have to add details (as in 1 below) but in most cases the subject on which you are asked to write serves as the beginning of a story or as a centre for the development of your ideas. The shape of the story is important: although it must be short, it should have a clear beginning, development and satisfactory end.

Conversation may form part of your story, especially if it is an essential part of the action.

Whether your treatment is formal or conversational will depend on how you tell your story. A report for a newspaper, for example, is likely to be treated formally; if however you wish to give the idea that you or someone else is telling the story, an easy conversational treatment would be more suitable.

Subjects

1 The postman delivers a letter which you open without looking at the name and address on the envelope. There is only a piece of paper inside with a message on it which seems to refer to some kind of criminal arrangement. You then realise that the name on the envelope is that of your very respectable neighbour. You take the letter to him and apologise for having opened it by mistake. Having read the message, the neighbour gives an unsatisfactory explanation of it. Write this story.
2 An elephant escapes from a small zoo and some of the animal keepers have to find it and bring it back. One of them relates what happens. Write his account.
3 Write a story in which somebody shows extraordinary courage.
4 Tell a real or imaginary story about how, when you were a child, you ran away from home, got completely lost and were found and brought home again.
5 Most people have dreamed of an experience which is most unlikely ever to happen to them. Describe some such unlikely dream experience.

The expression of opinions

General advice

Think carefully around the subject you choose and make notes of any useful ideas.

Several of the following subjects could best be developed in two paragraphs (for example: *for* and *against* as in 2 and 3) though a third general paragraph may be added. Otherwise try to group your ideas into three (with the possibility also of two or four) paragraphs.

Only general ideas can be dealt with in the number of words allowed.

Verbal shortenings and other spoken forms are not usual in this type of composition.

An example of this type of composition

Why do you think some people find it easier to learn a foreign language than others?

Plan: 1 Introduction: contrasting examples.
          2 Motivation, environment and teaching.
          3 Personal abilities

    I have met many British people who, after living several years in another country, speak hardly a word of the local language. In contrast there are those who somehow 'pick it up' and speak fluently within six months.

    Motivation is one of the most important considerations. Anyone who has to speak a new language in order to survive (or make money) will make a real effort, concentrating on listening and learning. The prospect of a better job or an examination or the wish to communicate with a new friend can have a noticeable effect. The good fortune of having an enthusiastic teacher is important, especially if the student is prepared to learn in his own time also.

    Memory plays its part — how quickly words escape from a poor one! Previous experience of language learning, together with intelligence of course, assist progress. And how much easier it is for the self-confident extrovert to practise newly-acquired expressions on native speakers of the language!

(160 words)

Subjects

1 Why would you enjoy *or* dislike being a school teacher?
2 Give the case both for and against the closing of all shops for two days together at week-ends.
3 What are the advantages and disadvantages of the extended family system of living together, that is to say a number of close relatives (grandparents, uncles, aunts, parents and children) living in the same house or very near to one another?
4 Why I enjoy (or would enjoy) owning either a car *or* a colour television *or* a dog, cat *or* other pet.
5 Explain *either* why you prefer to do your shopping in a supermarket *or* why you prefer to do it in one or two small shops.
6 What suggestions would you make for dealing with hooliganism (violent behaviour) at football matches?
7 Suggest reasons why so many holidaymakers prefer to spend most of their time on the beach.
8 What advice would you give to parents about the amount of pocket-money they allow to teenagers who are still at school?

A talk or speech

General advice

First gather and arrange the three or four main points you intend to develop.

    This is a talk, so verbal shortenings and other spoken forms will be used. As far as possible try to express your ideas in a way that is suited to the age and interests of your audience, who may be children, young people, the general public and so on, according to the instructions in the question.

An example of a short introductory speech

As chairman of a society interested in the arts you have to introduce a speaker who is a specialist in some aspect of art.

Plan: 1 Welcoming the audience.
2 Introducing the speaker.
3 Introducing the subject matter to be dealt with.

Good evening, ladies and gentlemen. I am very happy to see that so many of you have been able to come this evening in spite of the weather as I know that our speaker will have plenty to say that will be of interest to all of us.

Miss Constantina Dorico, whom we are delighted to have with us, has devoted several years to an intensive study of Byzantine art in Sicily, in particular during her four years of lecturing in the University of Palermo. She has travelled widely in Greece, Bulgaria and Italy gathering material for the book she is now preparing for publication. She is an expert photographer and has herself prepared the many beautiful slides that will be used to illustrate this lecture.

Miss Dorico will be speaking this evening on the main influences of Byzantine painting on pre-Renaissance art in Italy and we are all looking forward to hearing about a subject about which I at least know little, but like all of us here would like to know much more.

(175 words)

Contrast this formal style of speech with a possible opening to the first subject below in which children are being addressed:

Hallo, boys and girls. Nice to meet you. Now, I'm going to start by asking you a question. How many of you have to cross a road on your way to school? Yes, I thought so. Everybody.

Subjects

1 You are addressing schoolchildren of seven to ten years old about safety on the road, giving advice about behaviour when walking to and from school and also about playing near roads.
2 You have to write a short paper to be delivered to every home about a few of the accidents that children may have in the home and how parents should guard against them.
3 As a visitor to Great Britain you have been asked to give a talk to a group of British students on two or three ways in which you think that people in your own land differ in interests, everyday life and customs, appearance, character and so on (you can choose among these subjects) from people in Britain.
4 An employee of your firm is leaving after years of service and is to be given a gold watch. A speech is to be made in which this person and his/her work is praised and wishes for his/her future happiness and continued relationship with the firm are expressed. Write this speech.
5 You have been asked by your teacher to give a two to three minute talk in class on any one of these subjects:
 (*a*) unidentified flying objects (such as flying saucers)
 (*b*) the Loch Ness monster or some other creature that little is known about
 (*c*) lucky and unlucky charms (small objects and numbers)
 (*d*) happenings that may suggest good or bad luck to come
 (*e*) fear of darkness and the unknown.

Prescribed texts

Questions are set on 3 books selected from a range of specially-edited classic, adventure and science fiction novels. They will demand a knowledge of the different characters and of what happens in the story (but not interpretation or criticism) and will provide an optional alternative to the four other questions of the types already explained. Only one of the prescribed texts needs to be prepared, as only one essay on a book may be attempted.

General advice

When reading: Make notes on the various happenings in the story, including the names of characters, grouping your notes under suitable headings.

Revise these notes, making sure of the order of events, shortly before the examination.

Remember, you do not have to answer this question if you prefer two of the alternatives.

Answering the question:
1 Probably your main problem will be to present your material within the number of words suggested and not to spend too much time on this answer.

Be prepared to summarise where necessary, mentioning only the essential points. Pre-examination practice in doing this is important.
2 Make a plan as for the other compositions, keeping to the scheme of two, three or four paragraphs.
3 You may remember some of the words and phrases you encountered in the book and be able to use these effectively. Don't forget, however, always to think in English without translating from your own language.

Paper 3   Use of English

Section A

This section usually includes four questions of differing types. The first question usually involves the filling of gaps in a passage of continuous prose (as illustrated in the four passages in 1 below) and the second a series of transformation exercises (as in 2 a–k). The nature of the other two questions may vary from paper to paper.

A wide variety of additional exercises is included here, any of which might appear on a paper; they all provide useful practice in finding alternative ways of expressing ideas.

Advice on question 1

In Paper 3, the choice of words to be inserted in the gap-filling exercise depends not so much on word meaning (as in the sentences in Paper 1 Section A) as on the relationship of the word to structure and usage.

These are some of the factors on which the choice of word may depend:

nouns	— countables and uncountables as related to an accompanying verb or inclusion or omission of an article
	— commonly confused nouns such as opportunity/ possibility
verbs	— uses of modal verbs (can/ may/ must/ should etc.)
	— verbal constructions involving gerund or infinitive
	— conditional and reported speech forms
	— commonly confused verbs such as rise/ raise realise/ recognise
	— reflexive or non-reflexive (affecting pronouns)
	— phrasal verbs
pronouns and adjectives	— who/ which/ that/ whose, one/ ones, some/ any/ none, much/ many/ little/ few
	— article or possessive adjective e.g. in my hand
prepositions	— in phrases e.g. in the sky, at this moment
	— following other parts of speech e.g. an interest in, arrive at/ in, angry with
adverbs	— adjective/ adverb distinction e.g. hard/ hard/ hardly, such/ so
conjunctions	— distinctions e.g. if/ even if/ in case/ although
word order	— e.g. adverbs of time
idiomatic expression	— e.g. I think so, Yes, I will

This summary suggests only a classification of some possibilities; many more examples could be given.

Exercises

1 **Fill each of the blanks in the following passages with one suitable word.**

Note: always read right through the passage before attempting to fill the blanks.

1 (a) While they were in the taxi _____(1) their way home from the station, Stephen began to feel _____(2) ill. With _____(3) head swimming and a feeling of intense weakness in his limbs, he sat _____(4) out of the window but not _____(5) the people _____(6) the streets. He felt sure that he _____(7) have _____(8) temperature. _____(9) wife, who had _____(10) him at the station, soon _____(11) his silence and asked him _____(12) he was. He _____(13) back and closed his eyes. 'A _____(14) strange,' he said, 'but I'm sure it won't _____(15).' She wanted to know how long it had been _____(16) he _____(17) eaten. '_____(18) night at eleven o'clock I had a sandwich but before that I _____(19) not had time to eat, not even lunch. I've spent the last two days _____(20) the new plans with people in so many different places that I've never been able to stop to eat.'

1 (b) If you _____(1) the _____(2) of travelling _____(3) space, would you dare to _____(4) advantage of it? Many of you might say, 'Yes, I _____(5),' and others, 'Well, I think _____(6) but my decision would depend _____(7) a lot of other things such _____(8) how long the _____(9) would take and living conditions during the flight.' _____(10) people really believe that within twenty years there will be regular passenger services to the moon with meals served by courteous cabin staff and all modern comforts _____(11) in-flight films. _____(12) many years _____(13) come, only people with exceptional fitness, courage, qualifications and character will be accepted for the difficult training. And as plans _____(14) more ambitious and distances _____(15), the danger and discomfort may well _____(16). How many of us would enjoy _____(17) a few months in a small space, never _____(18) a normal meal, seeing always the _____(19) two or three people and never walking on good solid earth _____(20) the blue (not black) sky above?

1 (c) After _____(1) the hotel visitors' book, I went straight up to my room which was _____(2) the third floor. No sooner _____(3) I closed the door than I _____(4) just _____(5) tired I was. And yet when I went to bed, I lay awake for hours before at last I _____(6) heavily asleep. And the dream I _____(7) then was far worse than lying awake worrying and despairing.

I was in a large building, not unlike the one where I would have to do the following day's examination. People were hurrying silently _____(8) all directions. A large notice stated that the English Examination _____(9) take _____(10) in Room 999. But where could this room be? Not _____(11) any staircase I followed a dark passage to the left which was quite deserted and seemed to go on for ever. It ended at a very solid black door behind _____(12) I could hear people _____(13) with one another _____(14) quiet but angry voices. If _____(15) I could ask them for _____(16) information! I tried _____(17) on the door to attract their attention but immediately the voices died _____(18) and although I hurt my hand in my efforts, nobody opened the locked door. I then attempted in vain to find my _____(19) back to the entrance hall but as I wandered helplessly, a deep accusing voice broke the absolute silence everywhere, and filled the now empty building. 'The examination is over. There is no _____(20) in your remaining here. You are too late. Too late. Too late.'

1 (d) _____(1) spring morning last year, I met an old schoolfriend, whom I had not seen _____(2) several years. In fact it had been such a long time that I hardly _____(3) this rather fat, cheerful, grey-haired man who hurried _____(4) me as soon as he _____(5) sight of me.

'It's Patrick, isn't it,' he said excitedly, as he seized my hand. 'How many years must it be _____(6) we last met?'

'Ten at least,' I replied. 'You came to the station to see me _____(7) when I _____(8) for America.'

'Indeed, yes. And now _____(9) to the newspapers you have made a fortune. It seems _____(10) life has been very kind to you but I must also congratulate you _____(11) your success _____(12) a writer.'

'And how about you?' I asked.

'Oh, I haven't _____(13) so badly,' he said. 'Let's have a drink.'

He led me into the bar of what was clearly an extremely expensive and well-run hotel and ordered drinks. 'What do you think _____(14) this place?' he asked. And then, without _____(15) for my reply, he went on, 'Do you remember my father? He was a poor man and a very strict _____(16) too, who didn't approve _____(17) anything or anybody, especially me, and because he couldn't provide me _____(18) money, he was always giving me free advice. Above all he warned me against _____(19) married, which, he said, I would never be able to afford, and anyhow he didn't trust my judgment. Which was just where he was mistaken. Not only _____(20) my wife beautiful, attractive and very sweet but she also owns two factories, a chain of jewellery stores and this very profitable and comfortable hotel.'

2 **Finish each of the following sentences in such a way that it has the same meaning as the sentence before it.**
Example: It was wrong of you to speak so unkindly to him.
You should _____
Answer: You should not have spoken so unkindly to him.

2 (a) 1 She called twice but got no answer.
She called twice without _____
2 They won't let you take that dog into England.
You won't _____

3   People say he has been married four times.
     He is _____
4   I could reach the top shelf only with difficulty.
     I had _____
5   The students' results should have given you a lot of satisfaction.
     You should have been _____
6   He is very tired. He can't do much more.
     He is too _____
7   He is still on his way here.
     He hasn't _____
8   It is better to do something badly than not to do it at all.
     Doing _____
9   They asked questions of many different kinds.
     They asked a wide _____
10 You can't carry this suitcase. It is far too heavy.
     This suitcase _____

2 (b) 1   It would not be advisable for you to go to work tomorrow.
            You had _____
       2   He changed a traveller's cheque so that he should not be short of money.
            He changed a traveller's cheque so as _____
       3   He tried in vain to reach his friend on the telephone.
            He was _____
       4   Running five kilometres a day in wet weather doesn't do you any good.
            It isn't good for _____
       5   He continued to work until he was eighty.
            He went _____
       6   I don't want to go for a walk. I feel a little ill.
            I don't feel _____
       7   The arrangement was for the building to be ready by now but it isn't.
            The building was _____
       8   He has an idea that he might buy a caravan.
            He is thinking _____
       9   It was your secretary's duty to remind you about that.
            Your secretary _____
       10 This house was almost certainly built before 1800.
            This house must _____

2 (c) 1   Type more slowly and then you will make fewer mistakes.
            You would make _____
       2   'Don't talk with your mouths full,' she said to the children.
            She told _____
       3   Aunt Jemima came last February and is still staying with us.
            Aunt Jemima has been _____
       4   Would you be very kind and help me down with that suitcase.
            Would you be so _____
       5   It is quite certain that he will come back tomorrow.
            He is _____
       6   He got someone to paint his garage.
            He had _____
       7   He tried the other door but found that it was locked also.
            He tried the other door only _____

8 'May I use your telephone?' he asked me.
He asked my _____
9 It is possible that you left your gloves on the bus.
You may _____
10 It was your duty to work all the time I was out of the classroom.
You should _____

2 (*d*) 1 She offered me some more cake.
She asked me if _____
2 You need not have spent so much time on it.
It _____
3 As he got increasingly angry, he walked more quickly.
The _____
4 He got the best marks in our class.
Nobody _____
5 People will just have to put up with these small discomforts.
These _____
6 Are you still attending school?
Haven't _____
7 I should like you to get out of my way.
I wish _____
8 Those trees were blown down by Saturday's high winds.
It _____
9 Getting up early is more difficult than going to bed late.
It _____
10 The only thing they did was to criticise.
They did _____

2 (*e*) 1 In spite of her probable fear of the dog, she went up to him.
Although _____
2 You were very silly to waste your money like that.
It _____
3 There's no hurry. It isn't late.
It isn't late so you _____
4 Perhaps he didn't know you were waiting for him.
He _____
5 Jane has suggested that her overworked father should take an assistant.
Jane is trying to persuade _____
6 The last election was in 1974.
There _____
7 Nobody had expected such a good performance.
The performance _____
8 They must have had to cancel the meeting.
The meeting _____
9 'I think Andrew is ill as it's several days since I last saw him,' said Francis.
Francis said that _____
10 He crossed the road so as not to meet me.
He crossed the road to _____

2 (*f*) 1 They may have got home already and be waiting for us there.
It _____
2 It's such a long story that I can't tell it to you now.
It's too _____

3 The inexperienced motorist increased speed only when the road ahead was quite empty.
Only _____

4 The decision to dismiss fifty men was not made by the manager.
The decision that _____

5 He hopes he can take part in the next performance.
He hopes to _____

6 He can't swim and he refuses to learn.
He can't swim, nor _____

7 It wasn't necessary for you to make all that noise when you came home.
You _____

8 I definitely mean to find out the truth of the matter.
It _____

9 A housewife usually gets up first and goes to bed last.
A housewife is _____

10 I said I was sorry that I had not warned him.
I apologised for _____

2 (g) 1 The men solemnly promised never to forget that terrible day.
The men solemnly promised that _____

2 She said that her own letter must be posted at once.
She wanted _____

3 Although they tried to keep quiet, they couldn't help making some noise.
In _____

4 Many replies to the police request for information have been received.
The police _____

5 He told Graham not to forget to telephone him the following day.
' _____

6 During his journey to York, he had a fierce argument with the ticket-collector.
While _____

7 It was widely believed that he had murdered his partner.
He _____

8 I saw him three weeks ago but I haven't seen him since that time.
I've _____

9 January was cold but it has been even colder in February.
February _____

10 He hid the two watches because he did not want to pay duty on them.
He hid the two watches so as _____

2 (h) 1 He sold his shares fearing some loss in their value.
He sold his shares in _____

2 As he gets older, he becomes more and more forgetful.
The _____

3 He doesn't usually arrive so early.
It _____

4 Both you and your dog look equally tired and hungry.
Your dog looks _____

5 There was too little time for us to see all the paintings.
    We hadn't _____
 6 The waiter suggested that she should try the chicken soup.
    The waiter advised _____
 7 The boatkeeper warned me about the hidden rocks.
    '_____'
 8 He will deal with this immediately after his arrival tomorrow.
    He will deal with this as _____
 9 He was angry because he had to work overtime.
    He was angry about _____
10 Suppose we stop and have a cup of tea?
    How _____

2 (i) 1 We've all got umbrellas with us in case it rains.
          We've all got umbrellas with us because _____
       2 He explained our route three times because he didn't want us to get lost.
          He explained our route three times so _____
       3 Nobody can say yet whether the plan has succeeded.
          It is _____
       4 I have never met anyone less intelligent than he is.
          He _____
       5 I am sorry you didn't bring your camera.
          I wish _____
       6 'Why didn't you tell me yesterday, Miss Marks?' said the manager.
          The manager asked _____
       7 He next explained their plans for the following year.
          He went _____
       8 But for the warning notice I saw near the old mine, I might have fallen down.
          If _____
       9 People say he has discovered a cure for old age.
          He is _____
      10 The last news about the explorers came six weeks ago.
          There _____

2 (j) 1 Writing one's own language is less difficult than writing a foreign one.
          It isn't _____
       2 It wasn't necessary for him to borrow any money as he had enough.
          He _____
       3 He could not explain his very recent action.
          He could not explain what _____
       4 From the way they spend money you would think they were rich.
          They spend _____
       5 It was Mark's intention for his son to take over the business.
          Mark had decided _____
       6 It was seen that the ship was in some kind of trouble.
          The ship _____
       7 He did not remember his key until after he had shut his door.
          Only _____

8 People write and draw on a blackboard.
A blackboard is used _____

9 His relations thought he was living in Crewe.
He _____

10 His secretary finds his writing difficult to read.
It _____

2 (k) 1 People have said that gold has been found in several places.
Gold _____

2 He tried the shop door and was surprised that it was already locked.
He tried the shop door only _____

3 He had no sooner entered the lift than it started moving.
No _____

4 There is nothing to gain by waiting any longer.
There is no _____

5 You may have been studying for a long time but you still have a lot to learn.
However _____

6 The time has come when I must give notice to my employer.
It is time I _____

7 This is by far the most expensive thing I have ever bought.
I have _____

8 Jill can probably give you some advice.
Jill should _____

9 What a pity you lost your temper!
If _____

10 I advise you to get his permission first.
You had _____

3 **The word in capitals at the end of each of the following sentences can be used to form a word that fits suitably in the blank space. Fill each blank in this way.**

Example

There is little **comparison** between his earlier and his later work. COMPARE

3 (a) 1 He has been able to clear himself of the _____ of dishonesty.   ACCUSE

2 Few people realise completely their early _____.
AMBITIOUS

3 He may have made an _____ but it is far from being a sincere one.   APOLOGISE

4 He has eight children, each of whom, he claims, is more _____ than the other seven.   TROUBLE

5 How much can you really learn about a person from his _____ in society?   BEHAVE

6 A lot of money is not always a _____ to the person who has it.   BLESS

7 Anyone working abroad has to pay a lot for the _____ of his goods to and from home.   CARRY

8 He is proud and modest at the same time: an unusual _____ of qualities.   COMBINE

9 He blamed his _____ to pass the test on his nervousness.   FAIL

10 Hearing a noise in my kitchen, I seized a heavy hammer and crept _____ downstairs. CAUTION

3 (b) 1 No _____ about the date of the next General Election has been made yet. DECIDE
2 The mother cat attacked the large dog fiercely in _____ of her kittens. DEFEND
3 Arrangements can be made for the _____ of newspapers to any house in this district. DELIVER
4 To my _____ there was no cheque in the envelope. DISAPPOINT
5 It is thoroughly _____ to try to cheat in an examination. HONEST
6 Most teachers are Government _____. EMPLOY
7 He avoided the _____ of a taxi by taking a bus to the station. EXPENSIVE
8 The three-week strike of the workmen has been a _____ to the completion of the bridge. HINDER
9 The room seemed to be filled with ash-trays, pincushions, shells and other objects of little _____. VALUABLE
10 The _____ of buying food forced him at last to look for work. NECESSARY

3 (c) 1 You have caused _____ by criticising his son's behaviour. OFFEND
2 The _____ of the word 'a' changes the meaning completely. OMIT
3 The children were warned against eating _____ berries. POISON
4 Most of that country's milk _____ are exported. PRODUCE
5 We shall discuss your _____ at our meeting tomorrow. PROPOSE
6 She takes a certain _____ in never asking her neighbours for help. PROUD
7 But what are his _____ for such a well-paid post? QUALIFY
8 He had no _____ of ideas but he could not express them clearly. SCARCE
9 He was the only _____ of the family who attended the funeral. REPRESENT
10 It is your _____ to take all letters to the post. RESPONSIBLE

3 (d) 1 He always keeps _____ for electricity payments for at least a year. RECEIVE
2 He tried to encourage an interest in _____ matters. SPIRIT
3 You have indeed a right to _____ but not to special favour. JUST
4 I've a _____ that you're trying to borrow some money from me. SUSPECT
5 The _____ of this district attracts many visitors. BEAUTIFUL
6 The plan to build a new bridge has not yet been given the Government's _____. APPROVE

	7	He must take things quietly as he suffers from high blood _____. PRESS
	8	The accident was largely due to your _____. CARE
	9	Who has to come _____ to school? FAR
	10	All _____ should be addressed to the manager. COMPLAIN

3 (e) 1 This small country has now lost its _____. DEPEND
      2 Little has been done yet to control the world population _____. EXPLODE
      3 The firm demanded his _____ when it was discovered he had accepted bribes. RESIGN
      4 A person will die if there is not a _____ supply of blood to the brain. CONTINUE
      5 His toothache was clearly causing him a lot of _____. COMFORTABLE
      6 With two gasometers and a large power station only a short distance away, my _____ is not a beautiful one. NEIGHBOUR
      7 The violent storm caused the _____ of several houses. DESTROY
      8 An evening at home with a book can be more _____ than one at a dull party. ENJOY
      9 The distant view of a number of factory chimneys suggested that we were nearing an _____ town. INDUSTRY
      10 The strike has lasted ten weeks and _____ this time a hundred men have been idle. THROUGH

3 (f) 1 Is there any _____ of hiring a boat? POSSIBLE
      2 A bee-hive is usually a scene of great _____. ACTION
      3 He has turned down an _____ to join the government. INVITE
      4 He had lost so much blood that he no longer had the _____ to walk. STRONG
      5 The rare ornament was of such a beautiful shape that they all expressed their _____ for it. ADMIRE
      6 His _____ are so long that they send his audiences to sleep. SPEAK
      7 _____ have been made to combine the two branches. ARRANGE
      8 He was such an extreme _____ that he could not believe any evil of his country. PATRIOTIC
      9 A spoilt child often grows up to be very _____. SELF
      10 The _____ admitted that what looked like a diamond was false. JEWEL

4 (a) **Complete the following sentences with an appropriate word for a form of EMPLOYMENT (earning money or spending time)**
      1 He has recently lost his _____ and is looking for another one.
      2 My cat's favourite _____ is watching birds.
      3 Isn't it about time you started doing some _____.
      4 At the end of a long and successful _____ in the theatre, he is now writing his memoirs.

4 (*b*) **Complete each of the following sentences with an appropriate word for a form of PAYMENT.**
1 The _____ for this course should be paid within the first month.
2 The annual club _____ has recently been increased.
3 Could you make a _____ to help in our work with handicapped children?
4 The bus conductor will come for your _____.

4 (*c*) **Complete each of the following sentences with an appropriate word for a form of TIME or SPACE BETWEEN**
1 After their three-year _____, the family are now reunited.
2 Unfortunately there's a considerable _____ between what I earn and what I spend.
3 After a short _____ to blow his nose, the speaker continued.
4 There will be a(n) _____ between the first and second acts.

4 (*d*) **Complete each of the following sentences with an appropriate word for a form of TALK**
1 The Prime Minister is making a(n) _____ on television tonight.
2 There was complete silence in the church during his inspiring _____.
3 Professor Prosser gave an interesting _____ on the art of Central Asia.
4 I overheard a fascinating _____ between two ladies on a train.

5 **Make all the changes and additions necessary to the following sets of words and phrases to produce sentences which together make up a complete text (a–c) or letter (d–f). Note carefully from the example what kind of alterations need to be made.**
Example: I/ apologise/ not/ reply/ earlier/ letter/ which/ must/ delay/ post.
Answer: I apologise for not having replied earlier to your letter, which must have been delayed in the post.

5 (*a*) **The following sets of words express Susan's plans for next Sunday. Make them into complete sentences.**
1 next Sunday / I / get up / early if / I / not / oversleep.
2 unless / it / rain / I / go / a walk / the park / before / I / have / breakfast.
3 after / I / have / breakfast / I / spend / an hour / work / the garden.
4 quarter to eleven / I / go / church / which / be / a street / near / my house.
5 few minutes / before two / I / set out / visit / my cousin / who / live / a farm / about an hour / journey / here.
6 she / live / there / ten years / 1967.
7 I / have / enjoyable afternoon / ride a horse / feed the chickens / and / pick / apples / the trees.

8 when / I / be / tired / I / catch / the train / home / bring / me / large basket / apples / and / dozen / eggs.

5 (b) **Make these notes of an accident into complete sentences.**
1. the accident / take place / last Saturday / few minutes / after four o'clock.
2. Mr. Felix Anselm / drive / Jetflash sports car / the Firchurch road / the north end / the village / Hillhurst.
3. he / leave / the village / three minutes / and / travel / speed of / one hundred and twenty kilometres / hour.
4. he / notice / a van / travel / slow / he / be so / he / make up / mind / pass / it.
5. he / signal / correct / and / move out / the right / the middle / the road.
6. before / move out / he / not notice / large car / wait / come out / side road / some distance ahead.
7. think / he / have / plenty / time, / driver / this car / start / turn / right / still some way / front / van.
8. but / Mr. Anselm / drive / so fast / there / be / not enough time / driver / get / across the road.
9. both / drivers / keep / heads / and while / Mr. Anselm / turn / quick / to the left / the road / in front of the van / other driver / move / rapid / possible.
10. however / side / Mr. Anselm's / car / just / touch / other car / and / his car / run / a field / without / harm / driver / but / damage the car / slight.
11. The driver of the other car / able / stop / almost at once / and the van driver / offer / Mr. Anselm / lift / the next garage.

5 (c) **The following word groups represent notes on a meeting of the committee of the Heston Heath Social Club. Afterwards the minutes (account) of the meeting were written up in the same ten sentences. Write these minutes, making all necessary changes and additions, in ten complete sentences.**
1. The minutes of the last meeting / took / place / seven o'clock / evening / 23rd February / read / and / approve / those present.
2. Mr. Charles Merry / ask / what / do / his earlier suggestion / free drinks / provide / committee members / their meetings.
3. The Chairman / regret / have to report / only / few / members / think / any drinks / should / serve / committee meetings.
4. This statement / result / long and heated argument / most / which / not / recorded.
5. Miss Clementine Peacock / want / the committee / organise / dance / beginning of March / raise / money / children's party.
6. The Secretary / point out / it / be / too difficult / make / such / arrangement / for less / two weeks ahead.
7. She / suggest / dance / may hold / April / if they / be / sure / people / attend / make / profit.
8. She also / report / they / have to / postpone / buy / more chairs / until all members / pay / their subscriptions.

9 For half an hour / committee / discuss / members who / fail / pay their subscriptions / and / agree / they / ask / pay / or / stop / attend / club.
10 The meeting / come / end / little / before / half past eight / with the Chairman / thank / all those present / their co-operation.

5 (*d*) **Mrs Morton is going on holiday for two weeks. Before leaving she writes a letter to the woman who helps her with the cleaning, giving advice and suggestions about what she would like done during her absence. Make any changes and additions necessary to produce this letter.**

Dear Mrs Field,
1 I want / open / all / windows / daily / air / house / thoroughly.
2 I / suggest / clean / floors / and / dust / furniture / twice / week.
3 You / have / better / buy / polish / if / not be / enough / left.
4 My cat / not / need / feed / as / neighbour / look / her.
5 If / you / like / spend / evening / watch / my television / not hesitate / do.
6 Please / be / kind / send on / letters / that / arrive / before you / come / morning.
7 You / mind / ask / milkman / start / leave / milk again / two weeks' time?
8 I / look forward / see / when I / come / home / end / this month.

Yours sincerely,
Mary Morton

5 (*e*) **Miss Sarah Terry, secretary of the Kemble Amateur Dramatic Society, is answering a letter which she has just found on calling at the Society's office. The writer of the letter has asked for information about the society but wonders if her age will make her unsuitable for membership.**

Dear Miss Marple,
1 I / apologise / delay / answer / letter / 5th September / which / arrive / three days / but / I / only just / find.
2 I / do / best / provide you / information / you / ask / our Society.
3 The Society / establish / ten years / and / then / enjoy / considerable success / present / light comedies.
4 We / soon / start / rehearse / comedy / new writer, Septimus Sable.
5 If you / like / consider / a part / this play / we / hold / auditions / here / Thursday and Friday evenings / seven o'clock.
6 You / prefer / assist / other ways / possibly / make / costumes / or / act / prompter.
7 So far / your age / concern / , while / most / our members / be / age of forty / several / be / much older / that.
8 We / be / delighted / have / opportunity / meet you / if you / be / free / drop in / one evening / this week.

5 (f) Janus March, manager of Trendy Toys Ltd, is being briefed by his secretary about a telephone call received during his absence the previous day. This had been from a certain Augustus May, who had left an address but no telephone number so Janus has to deal with the matter in writing. The following word sets suggest the contents of the letter and should be suitably changed and added to so as to form complete sentences.

Dear Mr May,
1. When / I / arrive / this morning / I / inform / you / telephone / post / advertise / last Saturday / 'Times'.
2. My secretary / tell / she / promise / I / write / you / as soon / I / return / abroad.
3. I / try / deal / points / you / raise.
4. We / not yet / can / make / decision / exact salary / which / depend / successful applicant / previous experience.
5. However / it / certainly not / be / less / what / he or she / pay / the moment.
6. He or she / be / responsible / large department / and / good knowledge / new developments / in toy-making / require.
7. I / must / warn / whoever / appoint / have to / willing / travel / at least / a third / year.
8. If / you / be / interested / apply / this post / we / like / hear / you / next Monday / the latest.

Yours sincerely,
Janus March

6 In the following conversations, the numbered sentences have been left incomplete. Most are questions. Complete them suitably. Read the whole conversation in each case before you answer the question.

6 (a) A radio interviewer is speaking to Mr Goldstone, a film director, who has just arrived in London.

Interviewer: Good evening, Mr Goldstone. We're delighted to have you with us in the studio.
Goldstone: And I'm delighted to be back here in London.
Interviewer: (1) How long ago ———
Goldstone: About two hours. I've come here straight from the airport. (2) I'm rather tired actually because in all I ———
Interviewer: Fourteen hours! But haven't you just come from New York?
Goldstone: Indeed no. From Alaska. I've been there for the past ten days and have only just left.
Interviewer: (3) May I ask what ———
Goldstone: You certainly may. Making a film there.
Interviewer: Please tell me more. (4) What ———
Goldstone: People working there today and their problems living in the far north.
Interviewer: (5) When do you think ———
Goldstone: We had hoped to finish it by late summer but a strike among the cameramen is delaying us right now.
Interviewer: (6) How long ———
Goldstone: Only a few days. Then I hope I can get back to work on the film.

6 (b) **Sam is talking to the sergeant in a police station.**

Sam: I see there's a reward for information about Bert Sykes. Well, I've just seen him.
Sergeant: Oh, have you. (1) Now first, before you say anything else, what _____
Sam: Sam Smith, 1 High Street, Manchester.
Sergeant: All right. (2) Now, where _____
Sam: Coming out of the 'George the Fourth'.
Sergeant: And where were you?
Sam: At the bus stop opposite. (3) I _____
Sergeant: Which bus?
Sam: The Number 3. If that matters.
Sergeant: (4) What _____
Sam: A black overcoat, grey trousers, black shoes. No hat.
Sergeant: Was he exactly like that photograph on the wall?
Sam: Very little.
Sergeant: (5) Then how _____
Sam: Because I'm his brother-in-law. My sister's unlucky enough to be married to him.
Sergeant: (6) Do you know if _____
Sam: No, she hasn't. Not recently. He hasn't been near her for months. And she doesn't want to see him either. The sooner he's behind bars, the better for everybody.

6 (c) **A bus full of tourists has stopped outside the gate of Bonnybank Castle.**

Guide: On your left, ladies and gentlemen, is Bonnybank Castle. It isn't open to visitors but perhaps you'd like to ask some questions about it.
A: (1) When _____
Guide: Between 1310 and 1325. By the Lanceville family as a matter of fact, who then lived there for the next four hundred years.
B: (2) Who _____
Guide: Now? Oh, the Hammermills.
C: (3) How long _____
Guide: For the past hundred and fifty years. The present owner however is the last of the family and he's now eighty.
D: (4) What will happen when _____
Guide: That I don't know. There may of course be some distant relative.
E: (5) How _____
Guide: Fifty-five, including four dining-rooms, two ballrooms, five drawing-rooms, three kitchens, thirty bedrooms — and just three bathrooms. Any more questions?
F: Yes, the only important one.
Guide: What's that?
F: (6) What time _____
Guide: Lunch? Oh, we're going to stop for lunch at the Lanceville Arms Hotel in ten minutes' time.

6 (d) **A railway booking office clerk is answering questions over the telephone. The answers are shown. Write the questions, numbering them as below.**

Clerk: Southchester Station Booking Office. Can I help you?
Caller: (1) _____

Clerk: To Manchester? Let's see. It's five past nine now. The next one leaves at nine-thirty.
Caller: (2) _____
Clerk: Well, there's one at ten-fifteen and another at eleven-five.
Caller: (3) _____
Clerk: The ten-fifteen? Just over two and a half hours. It gets to Manchester at twelve-fifty.
Caller: (4) _____
Clerk: No, no dining-car on the ten-fifteen. There's one on the eleven-five, though.
Caller: (5) _____
Clerk: Nine pounds seventy-five second class.
Caller: (6) _____
Clerk: The ten-fifteen leaves from Platform 5.
Caller: (7) _____
Clerk: The last train back to Southchester tonight leaves Manchester at nine-thirty.
Caller: (8) _____

7 (*a*) **Write out the following passage in dialogue form. Begin as shown below the passage.**

Corporal Lucas returned to the camp after his week's leave a day late. He reported to Captain Wright and apologised for his lateness. Wright wanted to know the reason for it. Lucas explained that his father had had an accident the day before while he had been in Liverpool. He had been knocked down by a car and taken to hospital. The police had telephoned Lucas's mother who had been ill for the past week. So Lucas had stayed with his mother until the early evening when they had heard from the hospital that the father's condition was not serious.

Although he expressed some sympathy for Lucas, Captain Wright wanted to know why he had not telephoned the camp the day before to report what had happened. Lucas started to give an explanation but almost immediately changed his mind and said he supposed he would have to tell the truth. His father really had been taken to hospital the day before as he had said but he was afraid this was only half the truth. He had missed the train from London the night before his father's accident and got home only after his mother had heard the better news from the hospital. But even if he had not missed the train, he would have had to stay with his mother until they had heard that his father was out of danger.

Lucas started to say how he had got a lift back to camp but Wright interrupted him sharply, expressing his lack of interest in Lucas's means of travel. He had returned a day late and for this he would not be allowed to leave the camp for a week besides doing extra guard duty. Lucas accepted this decision and was dismissed.
Begin:
Lucas: Corporal Lucas reporting, sir, returning from leave. I'm sorry that I'm a day late.
Wright: Why are you so late?

7 (*b*) **Write out the following passage in dialogue form. Begin as shown below the passage.**

When Adam complained about the noise the people in the flat above were making again, his wife Sheila fully agreed. She admitted that they seemed quite pleasant people and probably had no idea that they were causing so much inconvenience. She suggested Adam's going up and telling them that she frequently suffered from nervous headaches and could not bear any loud noise.

Adam was not sure that calling on them just then would be a good idea and wanted instead to write them a polite letter.

Just then the radio was turned up causing even more noise. Sheila expressed her opinion of this very angrily and tried to persuade her husband to take this opportunity of complaining: the people would have to admit they were being a nuisance at that moment.

Adam hesitated and started to refuse but when his wife again urged him to go, he accepted her suggestion, straightened his tie, confessed he was not looking forward to what he was about to do and went upstairs.

Begin:

Adam: What a terrible noise those people upstairs are making again!
Sheila: Yes, aren't they? Even more than usual. Yet, they seem. . . .

7 (c) **On telephoning his wife, Mortimer Miggs found only his son Michael at home so he asked Michael to pass on to Mrs Miggs when she came home exactly what he had said. Michael did this, passing on to his mother in reported speech form everything that had been said, apart from his own opening words. Suggest what Michael said to his mother in reporting this telephone conversation.**

	Michael:	4321. Michael Miggs speaking.
1	*Father*:	Michael, ask your mother to come to the telephone for a moment.
2	*Michael*:	She can't. She isn't here just now.
3	*Father*:	Where is she? Has she been gone long?
4	*Michael*:	I don't know; she didn't tell me. She left about ten minutes ago.
5	*Father*:	Did she say when she'll be coming back?
6	*Michael*:	No, she didn't. But I don't expect she'll be long. She didn't take her shopping basket with her.
7	*Father*:	I wonder where she's gone. I must speak to her.
8	*Michael*:	What do you want to say to her?
9	*Father*:	Don't on any account post the letter I gave her. I've discovered I put the wrong letter into the envelope.
10	*Michael*:	Dad, I've just remembered why she went out. It was to post your letter.

Dad telephoned while you were out.
1 He told me _____
2 I said _____
3 He wanted to know _____
4 I said _____
5 He asked me _____
6 I told him _____
7 He said _____
8 I asked him _____
9 He asked me to tell you _____
10 I said _____

8   **The gaps in the following thirty sentences should be filled by the least possible number of words that will allow the sentence to make sense.**

8 (a)
1. He kept walking up and down so as _____ asleep.
2. It's no _____ blaming me. I had nothing to do with it.
3. If you hadn't insulted him, he _____ his temper.
4. We are looking forward _____ dinner with you next week.
5. Take a key with you _____ we are all out when you come home.
6. Shall I get you a cushion? Yes, please _____
7. He _____ a cigarette but I refused it.
8. What _____! First thunder, then rain, then snow and now this violent wind.
9. He drives his sports car _____ he were on a racing track.
10. I should like to _____ afford to buy a washing machine.

8 (b)
1. The committee members will meet as soon _____ agreed on a convenient time.
2. Don't you remember _____ that same mistake in your last homework?
3. I wish I _____ little more money.
4. Would you be so kind _____ me to move this furniture?
5. They asked me which shop _____ my dress material at.
6. They _____ of stealing but he denied this accusation.
7. The sun, which has just set, _____ for ten hours today.
8. 'What _____ all evening?' 'I've been playing cards.'
9. He suddenly realised that he _____ his cheque-book in his office drawer.
10. May I pay _____ these chocolates or is it the other assistant who takes the money?

8 (c)
1. _____ a flat in town, he has a small house in the country and a holiday home in Spain.
2. I hope her headache won't prevent _____ this afternoon's committee meeting.
3. Although he _____ the town for a year, he still doesn't know where the Town Hall is.
4. Now he has a camera he spends a lot of time _____ wild life.
5. Must you beat the carpets today? I'd _____ you did them tomorrow.
6. Dick's employer makes _____ overtime three evenings a week.
7. He still had on the overcoat he _____ in the street.
8. I was amused to see my cat Miranda _____ face carefully after she had drunk the cream.
9. If you _____ so much, you wouldn't be so fat.

10 He has such _____ that he has no idea how to spend it all.

9 **The words underlined in the following sentences can be replaced either by the word(s) in brackets or by an expression containing this word. Certain other changes in the sentences may have to be made.**
Example: I don't believe he is opposed to appointing an older person.   (OBJECTION)
I don't believe he has any objection to appointing an older person.

1 Carrying heavy weights is nothing new to him.   (USED — word order change)
2 The policeman told me I had driven too fast and without due care.   (ACCUSE)
3 Would you enjoy playing tennis now?   (FEEL)
4 Nobody can explain why all that money has been lost.   (ACCOUNT)
5 He waited until he had more certain information before he wrote to us.   (POSTPONE — word order change)
6 Everybody is quite sure he will be successful in the competition.   (BOUND TO)
7 The dry weather will mean that there won't be enough fruit for us this autumn.   (SHORT OF)
8 We asked him if we might leave early.   (PERMISSION)
9 We had expected them to be annoyed.   (SURPRISED)
10 He disliked all women doctors although he had no reason for this.   (PREJUDICE)

10 **Replace the lines in the following sentences with suitable conjunctions from this list:**

although, provided, in case, since, unless, whenever, as if, so that, if, until

1 He put up his umbrella _____ he shouldn't get wet.
2 _____ he was quite ambitious, he refused to study for higher qualifications.
3 Surely he won't be punished _____ he isn't guilty.
4 Discipline has become far less strict _____ I was at school.
5 You should be able to reserve a seat quite easily _____ you apply for it promptly.
6 I decided not to argue with the policeman _____ he should get angry with me.
7 He behaved _____ he owned the place.
8 His invention will never be developed _____ somebody provides the necessary money.
9 People continued to wave _____ they were too far apart to see one another.
10 _____ he visits a churchyard he pays special attention to what is written on gravestones.

Section B

This section consists of an exercise which requires the gathering together of information set out in one of various forms which include notes, and presenting it in well-constructed paragraphs, possibly giving reasons for or opinions about the information that is recorded.

General advice

Preparatory work on the answer

If time allows, you should spend about ten minutes (more if you have enough time) in preparing your answer on rough paper. This preparation will include selecting and arranging the information you will need, together with your own ideas if these are required. While there may not be time to write out the complete paragraphs in rough, you should at least have some idea before starting to record your answer on the examination paper whether you will be able to express your answer in the approximate number of words at your disposal.

(Above all, make absolutely certain that at the end of the examination you are not left with prepared material in rough which you have not had time to copy out on the paper. If this does happen, hand in your rough work with your paper.)

Understanding the instructions and material presented

Do not rush at the question. Read through the instructions two or three times so that you are quite clear about what you are being asked to do. Then read the information given slowly and carefully, making sure you understand what it involves and the connection between instructions and material. If you fail to do this, you may produce a completely inappropriate answer which will not be accepted.

Selection and arrangement

It is quite possible that not all the given material will be needed in your answer, or some of the less important items may have to be ignored to allow enough space in the given length for ideas of your own that may have been asked for. You must therefore consider carefully what can and should be included.

Having decided on the material you will include, you then have to arrange it in the order that will be most logical and effective.

Presentation

Sentences
The material should normally be presented in complete sentences which are so arranged as to form well-constructed paragraphs.

Vary the pattern of the sentences and also avoid the monotonous repetition of the same kind of construction such as 'there is/there are' and the constant use of 'to be — is/are' as the main sentence verb.

Vocabulary
Some of the vocabulary will be the same as that in the material given, but remember that the examiner wants to assess your own knowledge of vocabulary: words and phrases. Try to make effective use of a varied range of vocabulary. On the other hand keep within the limits of your language ability: your style should be clear, correct and natural as well as varied.

Remember — as always — not to translate from your own language.

Length

You may find it difficult to express all the information and personal ideas you think important in the recommended number of words. Compression — expressing a lot in a few appropriate words — is important and this is something you may need a lot of practice in before attempting the examination. You will also need practice in deciding which facts and ideas are essential and which, being of secondary importance, you may have to omit.

Note that the number of paragraphs required in answers to questions may vary. When four paragraphs are asked for, the approximate number of words in each may be 50.

Reading through   As in all parts of the written papers, this is absolutely essential. It is amazing how many mistakes even a highly-experienced writer will find on reading through a second time.

An example of this type of exercise

George Smith, an elderly man who has been living alone, now faces an important decision about his future. Information about three possibilities is given below. Having made his decision, George writes to his daughter in New Zealand suggesting his reasons.

Using the information given, continue each of the paragraph openings suggested underneath, stating his reasons for and against in about 70 words in each case. Add a final sentence in which he states his decision.

George Smith, aged 78, lives by himself in a bungalow in the suburbs of a small town. His health is reasonably good but now arthritis is making walking very difficult. He has a large enough pension to live on.

He is a retired headmaster who enjoys reading, music, cooking and watching TV and prefers a quiet life. He has a son, Mark, and a daughter, Anne.

He can now accept one of the two offers of accommodation referred to in 2 and 3 below, or he can continue as he is now. He has had a month to decide.

Possibilities:

1   His present home
    This is in a ground-floor flat with two rooms and kitchen and a telephone. A woman comes in to clean for him and do shopping every third day. He has a dog who can run freely in the communal garden.

2   The Lotus Valley Rest Home
    Situated in a large garden in the country.
    Accommodates 16 elderly and partially handicapped men and women.
    Accommodation: large, comfortable, communal lounge with TV,
                    smaller communal sun-lounge for reading, playing chess or cards
                    well-cooked meals served in dining-room
                    friendly staff of a married couple and two women
                    medical attention easily available
                    would share his bedroom with another man
                    no pets allowed.
    George's son and daughter would help to pay costs.

3   His son's home
    A terraced house near the centre of a large town.
    His son is married and has four children, between 10 and 17.
    His daughter-in-law, who is about 50, is sensible and reasonably friendly; she would accept but not really welcome him. She would not have the dog.
    A fair-sized bed-sitting-room would be available for him on the first floor and meals could be served there.

He could bring his TV, favourite chair and pictures and his books with him.

Paragraph openings:
If I move to the Lotus Valley Rest Home, _____
If I decide to live with Mark _____
In my own home _____

Suggested answer

(You may also wish to prepare your own answer to this exercise.)

If I move to the Lotus Valley Rest Home, I shall have a comfortable home and garden. I can read and watch TV, possibly not always my favourite programmes however. My meals will be prepared for me, though I shall miss cooking for myself. There will be company of my own age and I need not worry about getting help if I'm ill. I shall dislike sharing a room and hate losing my dog. *(74 words)*

If I decide to live with Mark, I shall have to put up with a lot of noise, both from the street outside and the children. I shall probably have to stay in my room on account of the stairs and this will be boring. My daughter-in-law will look after me well, even though she's not very friendly. I shall enjoy having some of my own things, but how about my dog? *(73 words)*

In my own home I shall find it increasingly difficult to look after myself. I do feel lonely there sometimes but I can spend the time quietly, doing the things I most enjoy. If I move I'll be a burden on other people, as you and your brother would have to help pay for accommodation in the Rest Home, or Mark's family would have to look after me. I know what my dog wants. *(74 words)*

I have decided to stay in my own home, at least for the time being.

(a) **The following descriptive details of four contrasting types of holiday appear in a brochure issued by the Faraway Horizons Holiday Company.**

   Below are the openings to four paragraphs. Complete each paragraph in about 50 words, explaining your preferences in order and giving reasons.

Paragraph openings
My first choice would be _____
My second choice would be _____
If no places were available on the above _____
I would on no account join _____

A
Where desert meets sea

This golden holiday offers you two weeks of fun and relaxation beside the sea in radiant North African sunshine
- a superb sandy beach with safe bathing, surfing, underwater exploration, boating
- accommodation in exotic two-roomed bungalows with cooking facilities
- a well-stocked supermarket on the site
- alfresco restaurant
- three discos and a night-club
- charter night flights at rock-bottom prices

B
Fitness fortnight for all ages

This activity fortnight provides:
- single person and family accommodation in a superbly-organised sports complex
- dining-hall, gymnasium, sauna, table-tennis and fitness rooms
- sports fields tennis courts and outdoor swimming pool
- instruction in many activities including rock-climbing, sailing, horse-riding, athletics
- organised rambles, pony-trekking, jogging
- TV lounges and bars for evening relaxation
- ample meals of natural health foods — special diets catered for

C
A family welcome in England, Wales, Scotland or Ireland

Would you like to get to know the people of the country you're visiting? And have the opportunity of practising their language?

Many families in holiday areas are happy to welcome paying-guests from abroad. They will provide:
- a comfortable single or double bed-sitting-room
- three good meals daily which you eat with them
- use of their sitting-room where you can talk together or watch TV
- family outings to places of interest
- all kinds of information about the locality
- friendliness and a wonderful welcome

Select your family from our illustrated information cards.

D
Scandinavian capitals tour

This tour includes:
- rail/sea travel from London to Oslo
- coach travel Oslo to Stockholm
- sea travel Stockholm to Helsinki and Helsinki to Copenhagen
- rail/sea travel from Copenhagen to London
- accommodation in four-star hotels
- Scandinavian breakfast, smörgasbord lunch, three-course dinner
- local English-speaking guides for the many excursions
- night-life tours in Stockholm and Copenhagen

2 nights in Oslo, 3 in Stockholm, 2 in Helsinki, 4 in Copenhagen.

(b) **Each of four university students lives in a different area of Riverville. Four paragraph openings are given below. Complete each paragraph, giving reasons why each student likes and/or possibly dislikes living in his or her particular area, using material from the information given about the town and its surroundings.**

Express their ideas in about 50 words in each case.

Riverville and its Surroundings

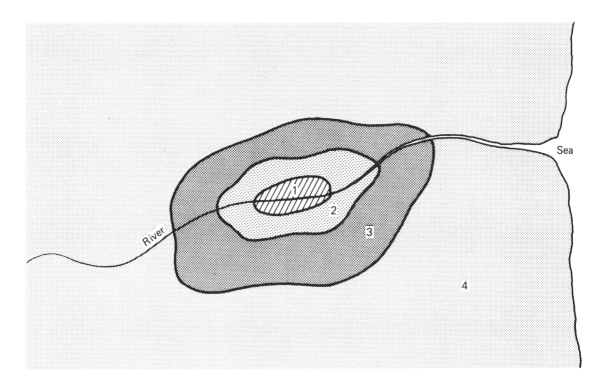

The town was established in the fourteenth century, largely as a result of the developing wool trade and home industry. The fine cathedral, Old Town Hall, Cornmarket and several other buildings, both civic and domestic, are between four and five hundred years old.

There was a rapid and unsightly expansion in the nineteenth century, due to industrialisation, when much of Area 2 was created.

Twentieth-century suburban development has spread over most of Area 3 and is now extending into the mainly countryside Area 4.

The four areas today

Area 1
A mixture of buildings from all periods in the town's history, including many multi-storey office blocks and public buildings.
  Excellent shopping facilities in a shopping precinct.
  Public buildings include the university, museum and art gallery, technical college, railway station and bus station.
  Narrow streets congested with lorries, buses and cars — inadequate parking facilities.

Area 2
An area of factories, small workshops and until recently slums, which are now being replaced largely by high-rise blocks of flats.
  Shops mainly for everyday needs, low-priced restaurants and snack bars. A lot of cafés, some cinemas and discos.
  Good bus services to the town centre.

Area 3
Mainly residential: streets of semi-detached houses with gardens or small blocks of flats.
  A variety of small shops, expensive Indian, Chinese and Italian restaurants, parks with sports facilities, branch libraries.
  Limited bus service: most residents drive to centre.

Area 4
Mainly rather pretty countryside with hills, farms and villages.
  Two hypermarkets and two large sports centres on main exit roads from town.
  Limited bus service: in most parts, one an hour on some roads only and none after 8 p.m.

The four students

Ann, Bob, Carol and Dick are all studying at the university in the town centre.
  Ann lives in a hostel near the university.
  Bob has a bed-sitting-room near the river in Area 2.
  Carol lives with her parents in Area 3.
  Dick is married and rents a cottage in a village some ten kilometres from the town centre.

Paragraph openings
Ann thinks that _____
Bob says that _____
Carol is quite sure that _____
Dick considers that _____

(c) You have been discussing with a private language teacher from whom you intend to take lessons those aspects of the learning of English you would like to pay most attention to. You have considered the various possibilities listed below and have noted down one or two reasons for and against spending time on them. Finally you decide on the four you consider most valuable to you personally, having regard to your own circumstances and objectives, and you write a four-paragraph report suggesting reasons for spending rather more or rather less time on each of the four.

Continue the paragraphs shown below the notes, using about 50 words in each case to express your ideas.

Possibilities

1 *A general study and revision of grammar, with particular attention to mistakes you make.*
   Practice in using grammar to express ideas.
   Is grammar necessary?

2 *Translation from and into English.*
   Usefulness in learning language?
   Do I need it in my job?

3 *Conversation on general topics.*
   Improvement in fluency and ease of expression?
   Can I learn anything new in this way?
   Enjoyment for its own sake?

4 *Planned conversation.*
   Discussion of article or topic prepared beforehand?
   Preparation time available?
   More or less useful than free conversation?

5 *Study of contemporary texts (from newspapers, magazines, modern literature, plays etc.)*
   Acquisition of up-to-date vocabulary and current ideas under discussion.
   Too passive?

6 *Listening comprehension.*
   Nature of material: broadcast talks, opinions, conversations?
   Making use of the material heard: testing? discussion?

7 *Writing.*
   Type of exercise: essay? letters? comprehension?
   Time available outside lessons?
   Value of writing in learning?

8 *Reading and discussion of a work of literature.*
   Am I ready for this?
   Value in learning?

Paragraph openings
I should like to spend most time _____
There is a lot to be gained from _____
I think it would also be useful _____
Finally, some time should be given to _____

Paper 4   Listening Comprehension

Advice

The recorded texts used for this part of the examination will include announcements, different types of situational dialogues and radio-type sequences of news or features.
The questions accompanying the passages will involve labelling pictures and completing charts as well as answering multiple choice exercises.
You should expect to answer questions on at least three passages during the test. Each passage will normally be heard twice.

Guidelines

1 Before you actually hear each recorded text, you will hear a brief outline of what the passage is about, together with detailed instructions on which questions on the exam paper you are to answer and in what manner. This will be followed by a short pause before the recording begins. It is very important to listen carefully to the recorded instructions and use the pause to look through the questions as closely as you can in the time available. They may mean little to you before hearing the passage, but certain clues about what to expect and to listen for in particular will be there.
2 When you first hear the recording, try to concentrate on the general subject matter. Even though you may notice the answers to some of the questions, do not be tempted to indicate these answers while the recording is playing as you may lose concentration and miss important points in the rest of the passage as a result.
3 After the first hearing, read all the questions again and answer the questions you are quite sure of. Now check through the unanswered questions, or the gaps in information you still have, in order that you know exactly what to give special attention to while listening to the recording for the second time.
4 After the second hearing, complete your answer sheet and check the correctness of the answers you have already given.
5 After checking through your answers a final time, you could start considering the questions on the next passage.
6 You will have a few spare moments before giving the papers in at the end of the examination, so use the time for final checking of difficult questions or for completing any still undecided answers. Remember not to leave any point unanswered as this will only lose you marks.

Exercises

1 **Krista Berg, who is staying for a short time in England, is interested in joining the Newmarket Public Library, so she goes to the library to enquire about membership. Complete the application form below.**

	BOROUGH OF NEWMARKET PUBLIC LIBRARIES APPLICATION FOR MEMBERSHIP
Name in full	( )
Address	
Occupation	
Age	
Nationality	
Signature	
Guarantor's Signature	

2 **On hearing the doorbell, Joan opens her front door and finds Terry, a door-to-door salesman, waiting outside.**

1 How does Joan behave when she sees the salesman standing outside her door?
   A She shows clearly her complete lack of interest in buying anything.
   B She shuts the door in his face.
   C She gets angry with him.
   D She tells him to go away.

2 What is her immediate reaction to the offer of a free gift?
   A She expresses her belief that it will have little value.
   B She shows no interest in the offer.
   C She wants to know whether she must buy something before she gets it.
   D She refuses to accept it.

3   The salesman's basket
    A   is very light so that he can carry it without difficulty.
    B   is so designed that he can show its contents easily.
    C   can be separated into two parts.
    D   has a very attractive appearance.

4   A customer can buy the things he wants by
    A   paying at once and getting the goods in a few days.
    B   examining the goods now available and buying them from the vanman.
    C   paying on delivery for what has been ordered from the salesman.
    D   buying immediately in the case of a single article carried by the salesman.

5   The washing-powder being offered by the salesman
    A   is cheaper and does not have to be carried home.
    B   is of better quality and cheaper than most others.
    C   is cheaper and specially prepared for washing machines.
    D   is easier to carry and also costs less.

3 **Marlene is speaking to her friend Gina on the telephone.**
   Answer each of these five questions by putting a tick (✓) opposite the appropriate response in the box below.

1 How often does Gina go to the cinema?

At regular intervals	
Now and again	
Most Wednesdays	
Every so often	

2 Which cinema did she visit the previous evening?

Regina	
Imperial	
Marshall	
Regal	

3 Which film did she see?

Sky Divers	
Night Riders	
Night Drivers	
High Gliders	

4 What was her opinion of the film? She found it

Excellent	
Fair	
Exciting	
Boring	

5 Where in the cinema did she sit?

In the centre	
At the front	
In the balcony	
At the back	

4 **Mrs Street has just come into the Featherfleet Shoeshop.
Complete each of these tables by putting a tick (✓) against each item
of information that applies to the shoes Mrs Street finally preferred.**

STYLE		COLOUR		PRICE		SIZE		FITTING	
Slippers		Brown		£20		36		Narrow	
Walking-shoes		Beige		£22		37		Medium	
Sandals		Black		£32		38		Wide	
Court shoes		Green		£39		39		Medium-wide	

5 **This is an extract from a short talk on food preservation that forms
part of a Woman's World radio programme.**

1 The general subject of this talk is
   A advice about storing cooked food in a refrigerator.
   B the maintenance of a refrigerator.
   C how to use your refrigerator.
   D keeping food fresh with the help of a refrigerator.

2 According to the advice given, which of the following will deteriorate in the fridge if not covered?
   A Milk.   **B** Vegetables.   **C** Cheese.   **D** Eggs.

3 What advice is given about the storage of food that has been cooked?
   A It should not be stored for too long.
   B It should no longer be warm when put into the fridge.
   C It should not be eaten without further cooking.
   D It should not need further cooking.

4 Why should you leave space between things in the fridge?
   A To avoid losing things.
   B To admit fresh air into the fridge.
   C To maintain an even temperature.
   D To ensure that the food has air around it.

5 How often should you defrost and clean the fridge?
   A At fixed intervals.
   B Now and again.
   C Whenever it needs it.
   D Whenever it seems too crowded.

6 **This advertisement might be heard on commercial radio.**
   The list below suggests twelve desirable qualities in a car. Put a tick (✓) against the five mentioned in the advertisement.

Low price		Four doors	
Low petrol consumption		Large windows	
Easy steering		Ample luggage space	
Long wear		Efficient braking system	
Smart appearance		Enough space for a family	
Easy maintenance		Four wheel drive	

7 **A local radio station has broadcast the following advice in its weekly programme for Senior Citizens.**

   1 Even with the travel permit a senior citizen still has to make some payment on
      A the London Underground.
      B all London Country buses.
      C Green Line buses.
      D London Transport buses.

   2 Permit-holders have to pay on buses
      A on Saturdays.
      B before 9.30 a.m. on Mondays.
      C after 7.30 on weekday evenings.
      D daily between 9.30 a.m. and 4 p.m.

   3 Which of these people would be entitled to a permit?
      A A sixty-two-year-old man resident in Westminster.
      B A seventy-year-old woman visiting from Scotland.
      C A woman of sixty-four living near Oxford Circus.
      D A seventy-four-year-old man confined to a wheel-chair.

   4 The applicant must provide proof of age if
      A he/she lives outside the Greater London area.
      B he/she is unable to provide photographs.
      C he/she is not applying to the nearest Post Office.
      D he/she does not draw a State pension.

5   A senior citizen can obtain a permit without having a pension book if
    A   a friend takes the documents.
    B   he/she makes special application on a Saturday morning.
    C   he/she is a visitor to London.
    D   he/she provides proof of age and residence besides two photographs.

8   **Estelle Hope is being interviewed for a post in a large London travel agency by the firm manager.**
    The list below suggests ten possible qualifications that the manager is looking for. He puts a tick (✓) against the five that Estelle appears to possess. Show by your own five ticks where you think these were placed.

Typing ability		Job interest	
Knowledge of a foreign language		Knowledge of London	
Good memory		Punctuality	
Availability for overtime work		Availability for long-term appointment	
Politeness		Previous experience in this type of work	

9   **This week Peter Pullet, a dentist, is giving a talk about dental care on the 'Home Health' radio programme. This is what he says about toothbrushes.**

   1   The speaker introduces his remarks about toothbrushes by
       A   stating some considerations buyers should have in mind.
       B   suggesting some unsatisfactory reasons for a choice.
       C   emphasising the importance of using a toothbrush.
       D   asking questions that he intends to answer later.

   2   Why are nylon filaments better than bristle?
       A   They dry more quickly.
       B   They last longer.
       C   They are more flexible.
       D   They keep cleaner.

   3   A multi-tufted brush is preferable because
       A   it doesn't hold water and go soft.
       B   it can destroy bacteria in the mouth.
       C   it can cover a wider area of the teeth.
       D   it can remove impurities more effectively.

   4   What does the speaker think of a hard brush?
       A   It can be more effective than a soft one.
       B   It does not need to be changed as frequently as a soft one.
       C   It can wear away the surface of the teeth.
       D   It does not clean the teeth thoroughly.

5   The speaker's opinion of the choice of an electric toothbrush is that
    A   this is a matter of personal taste.
    B   they are more efficient in most ways than ordinary ones.
    C   they should not be used by elderly and less capable people.
    D   they make effective cleaning easier.

10 **Susan and Martin are having tea and buttered toast in front of the fire on a Sunday afternoon.**
    The presents shown below are all mentioned in the conversation between Susan and Martin. Show the five they actually decide to give by putting a tick (✓) in the appropriate boxes.

11 **Mrs Drudge is visiting the doctor.**

1 Emily Drudge visits her doctor
   A regularly.
   B once a year.
   C occasionally.
   D as soon as she feels unwell.

2 What is the matter with Emily now?
   A She is completely exhausted.
   B She is unable to continue her job.
   C She has little energy or interest in life.
   D She can't eat or sleep.

3 What does Emily say about her eating habits?
   A She has no interest in food.
   B She can't afford to eat properly.
   C The food available has to be given to her family.
   D She hasn't much opportunity of eating properly.

4 What information does Emily give about her husband?
   A He is still suffering from the effects of the war.
   B He does no work.
   C She has to do everything for him.
   D He is constantly in poor health.

5 Emily didn't go away during her last holiday because
   A she hadn't enough money.
   B she had to work most of the time.
   C the weather was too bad.
   D they had to make a number of visits.

12 **Lorna is in a tourist information office asking about accommodation. The tourist office clerk completes this form by putting a tick (✓) in one appropriate box in each column. To show what accommodation Lorna eventually chooses, show where she puts them.**

TYPE OF ACCOMMODATION		TYPE OF ROOM		MEALS		POSITION OF ACCOMMODATION		PRICE	
Four-star hotel		Single		No meals		In the centre		£8	
Two-star hotel		Double (1 bed)		Bed and breakfast		Near the park		£18	
Boarding-house		Double (twin beds)		Half-board		In the suburbs		£23	
Private house		Double and extra bed		Full-board		On the outskirts		£28	

13 **Mr Ken Crook is being questioned at a police station by a sergeant. (In choosing your responses, you should assume that Crook is telling the truth.)**

1 Crook was unwilling to answer the questions again because
   A he had given all the information he could already.
   B he wanted to go home.
   C he was afraid of contradicting himself.
   D he didn't understand why he was being questioned.

2 How did Crook know Mr White's address?
   A Mr White bought things from Crook's firm quite often.
   B The two men worked for the same firm.
   C The firm kept records of their more frequent customers.
   D Mr White lived very near Crook.

3 Crook wanted to get in touch with Mr White in order to
   A ask him what to do about his car.
   B tell him what was wrong with his car.
   C get his permission to carry out repairs.
   D tell him his car could not be mended yet.

4 When he was in the flat he discovered that
   A there had been a burglary.
   B the furniture had been damaged.
   C Mr White had been attacked.
   D the flat was empty.

5 How did Crook discover the condition of the room?
   A He turned on the light.
   B He felt his way around.
   C He carried his own light.
   D He could see from the light in the hall.

14 The Lost Property Office clerk is more than usually busy today. Put a tick (✓) in the box beside each of the five lost things referred to in the passage.

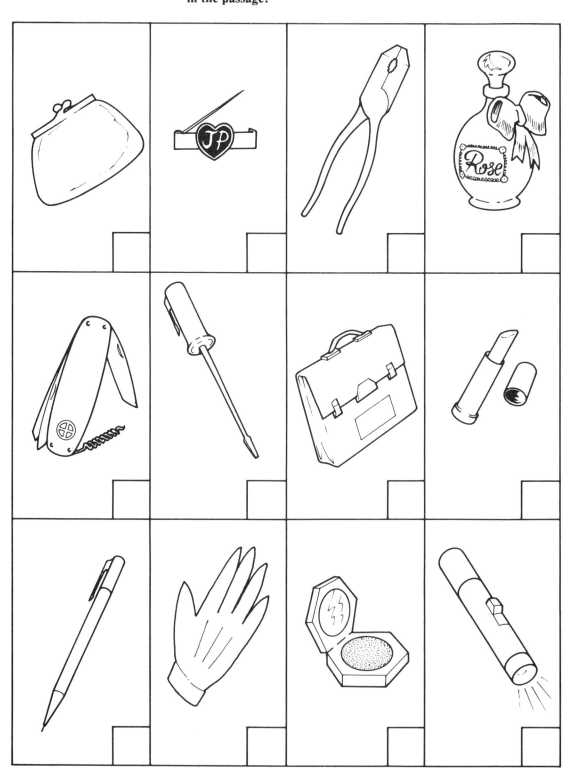

15 **Laura and Henry are discussing the arrangements for their daughter's wedding reception.**

1 In which of these ways are Henry and Linette in agreement about the wedding reception?
   A   It will be expensive.
   B   Neither of them wants one.
   C   Linette's opinion should be asked on the matter.
   D   It's too far in the future to bother about yet.

2 What argument does Laura use to win over Henry's support?
   A   Henry likes organising things properly.
   B   The reception could be a means of maintaining useful business contacts.
   C   She has a very high opinion of his advice.
   D   He could invite some of his business colleagues to the reception.

3 Where do they finally decide to hold the reception?
   A   At home.
   B   In the Church Hall.
   C   In the Grand Hotel restaurant.
   D   At the Golf Club.

4 Another responsibility for the arrangements that Laura volunteers to take on is
   A   deciding which people should be invited.
   B   sending out the invitations.
   C   ordering the invitations.
   D   inviting the Vicar.

5 Why does Henry break off the conversation?
   A   He does not want to be involved in choosing the bridesmaids.
   B   He always spends Saturday afternoon at the Golf Club.
   C   He wants to show his opposition to the reception.
   D   He does not want to be involved in discussing the dresses.

16 This is an extract from a radio programme about gardening.
    Ten things that may or may not be useful in the creation of a rock garden are listed below, but only five of them are implied as essential in the passage. Place a tick (✓) in the box that follows each of the five.

Patience		Trees to give shade	
A sloping site		Damp soil	
A place which gets the sun		Freedom from unwanted plants	
The right season of the year		A fair amount of strength	
Sufficient free time		Natural surroundings	

17 This is a loudspeaker announcement to customers in Fashionfare Department Store.

   1 Why have the police asked the car-owner to remove his or her vehicle?
      A It is blocking the traffic.
      B It could cause difficulty in an emergency.
      C Parking outside the shop is forbidden.
      D They don't want the trouble of taking it away themselves.

   2 What will the pop singer be doing in the Teens and Jeans department?
      A Selling ski-outfits.
      B Signing records.
      C Opening a sale there.
      D Taking part in a fashion show.

   3 The firm hopes that the visit of the Scream group's soloist will result in an increase in sales of existing stocks of
      A jeans.
      B swimsuits.
      C ice-skates.
      D records.

   4 What is one of the attractions of the fashion show?
      A Customers can see there the new range of available fashions.
      B Some very good bargains will be shown.
      C It will feature the latest ice-skating outfits.
      D Customers can get useful ideas about fashion holiday wear.

   5 When is the stock-taking sale to start?
      A In half an hour.
      B Next Tuesday.
      C Tomorrow.
      D At four o'clock.

18 Maureen has dialled the number of the Checkpoint Repair Service. As he listens, the manager fills in details on the form below. Complete it as he does.

CHECKPOINT GARAGE BREAKDOWN SERVICE	
Customer's name	
Location of car	
Damage or fault	
Time at which reported	
Car model	
Registration number	

19 **Jeremy is ringing the Willingservice Electrics shop.**

1 What is the first piece of information the manager asks for?
   A The reason for the call.
   B The name of the speaker.
   C What has gone wrong.
   D The type of television involved.

2 Why is Jeremy ringing Willingservice Electrics?
   A He bought the set there.
   B They are the makers of these sets.
   C He has been advised to do so by the sellers.
   D This is his nearest repair firm.

3 What is wrong with the set according to Jeremy?
   A The picture only is not clear.
   B At times both sound and picture are distorted.
   C Occasionally he cannot get one of the programmes.
   D The aerial he has is unsatisfactory.

4 A mechanic cannot be sent for some days because
   A the firm never employs more than one or two people.
   B one or more of the employees is absent from work.
   C this is a particularly busy period.
   D the firm is unwilling to do the job.

5 What is Jeremy's reaction to the suggested arrangement for calling?
   A He is angry about it.
   B He does not find it very satisfactory.
   C He would like them to call later on Tuesday.
   D He feels sure it will not be carried out.

20 Mrs Morley has bought some new furniture for a bungalow she is moving into, and she wishes it to be delivered there before her other furniture.

She is telephoning the firm she has bought the furniture from and, as she can't be at the bungalow herself, is giving instructions about where each item should be placed.

Draw a box with the appropriate letter in it in each of the places where the furniture should stand. Box A is already shown in position as an example.

A	B	C	D	E	F
cooker	armchair	desk	wardrobe	bookcase	laundry basket

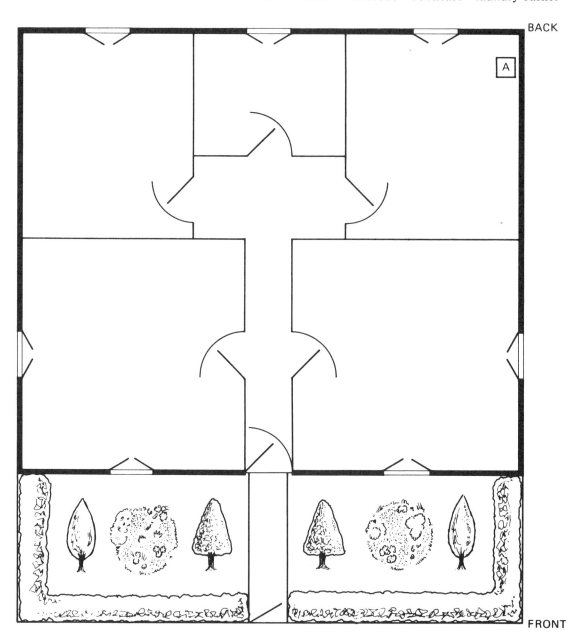

Paper 5 Interview

Conversation based on photographs

Advice

Three common faults that oral examiners are aware of are:
1 an inability among candidates to develop ideas both about the subject matter of the picture itself and in the following general discussion.
2 lack of organisation in the ideas put forward.
3 the use of a very limited vocabulary and sentence pattern. In many cases the candidate has the ability to express himself more fluently and effectively but lacks practice in making the most of his knowledge and/or is too nervous and self-conscious to do so.

All these faults could be remedied by pre-examination practice.

1 Ideas

Common general aspects of the subject-matter of pictures could be considered beforehand, e.g.
a) Descriptions of people:
— what they look like; general build, hair, special items such as a beard or glasses, facial expression
— what kind of clothes they are wearing, possibly in relation to the apparent personality of the wearer
— the general impression of the person described: he/she may seem worried, annoyed, cheerful, efficient, depressed, amused by something
— not only *what* he/she is doing but also *how*

b) Descriptions of places and/or a person's surroundings.
These may include scenery, buildings, streets, and scenes of activity such as an airport, a market-place, a football match, or a procession.

c) Descriptions of activity including those happening at the places mentioned above and accounts of the actions going on: a photograph of a person making a telephone call may involve an account of what happens when a person makes a call.

2 Organisation of Material

An examiner may ask questions about a picture or merely ask the candidate to describe one, so practice in free description is needed.

The various ways of organising the material in the latter case may include a decision as to what is the main subject of the picture (possibly a person), describing this subject first and then fitting the subject into its surroundings.

Another approach could be a consideration of the picture in areas: 'Most of the foreground of the picture is occupied by . . .'

Organisation and logical development are essential qualities in picture description.

3 Vocabulary and Sentence Structure

An oral examiner can sometimes recognise that a group of candidates have been trained in making an intelligent use of structural variety in expressing themselves.

A very few of the many useful expressions that could be introduced are:
— I have the impression that . . .
— I think it can be taken for granted that . . .
— From the expressions on their faces I'd suggest . . .
— One of the most striking features of this picture is that . . .

Remember, however, to think in English and avoid any kind of translation from your own language: the expressions you introduce should be ones you know you can use effectively.

Picture 1

1. Describe the girl's surroundings.
2. What impressions have you got of the girl herself?
3. Suggest some reasons why she has stopped working.

Topics

Some of the duties of a secretary.
Why you would or wouldn't like working in an office.
Some of the advantages and disadvantages of having pot-plants in one's workplace or home.
The advantages of having a cheerful personality.

Picture 2

1. What are some of the things these women have been doing since they entered the shop ten minutes ago?
2. In what ways are the two women shoppers at the desk alike and different?
3. Describe various things you probably have to do when you want to pay for your goods in a self-service shop.
4. Suggest why chocolate or bags of sweets are displayed just above the cash-desk.

Topics

Some advantages and disadvantages of supermarket shopping.
Why do some people prefer to buy things in a small counter-service shop?
Why do a lot of people enjoy window-shopping?

Picture 3

1. Describe the little boy: what he looks like, what he's wearing and what he's doing.
2. What are your impressions of the room?
3. Compare this room with the living room in your own home.

Topics

Some of the pleasures and problems of looking after a small child.
Some of the advantages of being a small child.
What are some of your ideas about bringing up and educating children?

Picture 4

1. Describe the surroundings in this picture.
2. Suggest various reasons for assuming that this photograph was taken during one particular season of the year.
3. Describe the various expressions on the cyclists' faces and suggest reasons for them.

Topics

Why do you think cycling clubs are popular with people of various ages? Give several reasons.

Suggest a number of ways of keeping fit in the open air. Which do you prefer and why?

In what ways can a bicycle be a very useful means of transport?

Picture 5

1. Describe the appearance and clothes of the woman in the picture.
2. What has she been doing? What is she doing now? What will she do when the food is cooked.
3. What various features of the photograph make it obvious that it was taken in a kitchen?

Topics

Why some people enjoy cooking and others find it a nuisance.
Your opinions about a man's place in the kitchen.
Give your views on the statement that the kitchen is the most important room in a house.

Picture 6

1 What details in the picture make it obvious that the students are doing an examination?
2 What are the various duties of the man in glasses?
3 What are some of the things you might hear in this room?
4 In what ways are these young people similar in appearance to those in your own country?

Topics

Give your ideas about the value of written examinations.
Advise a student who is nervous about an exam he has to take in a few days' time.
Suggest an effective answer to someone who considers that cheating in an exam is clever or in any way excusable.

Picture 7

1. Give an exact description of the body position of any one person taking part in the exercise.
2. Suggest some other forms of activity that this gymnasium is equipped for.
3. What other exercises might the instructor ask the boys to do as part of this routine?

Topics

Suggest some forms of physical activity that older, possibly retired, people can enjoy.

To what extent did (or do) gymnastics, outdoor games and sport in general form part of your school curriculum?

What arguments might you use in an attempt to persuade an adult who prefers an indoor life to take up some form of physical activity?

Picture 8

1 Describe what you can see in the background of this picture.
2 Describe what you can see of the appearance of each of the four girls.
3 Judging by the expressions on their faces, suggest what they might be talking about.

Topics

Café life in your own country.
Why people of various types (including students, businessmen and housewives) enjoy a break together for a drink.
Describe a typical small, low-price café.
Arrangements made by schools and firms in your country for the provision of a midday meal for pupils or employees.

Note: The letters LV in the photograph indicate that Luncheon Vouchers are accepted. These are issued by some firms to their employees and can be exchanged in certain restaurants as payment or part-payment for a meal.

Reading a Passage

Advice

1. You will probably be asked to define the subject of the passage. This is usually fairly obvious and your answer could be expressed in such words as:
   — From the use of the words —— and ——, it seems probable that . . .
   or:
   — I'd suggest that the passage is dealing with / describing / explaining . . .
2. You will be given a few moments to look through the passage before reading it aloud. As you look through, pay special attention to points that may show up your special weaknesses in reading aloud.
   These may include:
   a) difficulties with certain sounds; you will know the sounds that cause you particular problems.
   b) syllable weakenings as in: particular /pətɪkjələ/
      word weakenings as in the sentence:

      / hɪ keɪm ət faɪv tə tu: ənd steɪd fə faɪv mɪnɪts /

      (He came at five to two and stayed for five minutes.)
   c) concatenation = the joining of a final consonant to a following vowel:
      a half-eaten apple   for over an hour
   d) intonation — especially in questions and exclamations.
   e) emphasis by means of intonation, pauses and voice.

Read *clearly* and *not too quickly*. Fast reading encourages mistakes and makes attention to finer points of weakening and intonation more difficult. It may also irritate the examiner as the over-fast reader is often hoping to hide his weaknesses or to give the impression of greater reading ability than he really has.

Reading passages

During the Interview the candidate is shown a short reading passage and asked to identify the speech situation it refers to. He/she then reads the passage aloud.
   The passage is likely to be of a type illustrated below.

1. First heat the grill for several minutes. Season the meat and place it on the grid of a grill pan. Brush over it a little melted butter, oil or fat, and cook rapidly for 2 minutes before turning it over and repeating the process. Lower the grill temperature and cook the meat more slowly until it is ready for the table.

2. For these reasons, your parcel needs to be securely packed and sealed — otherwise it could become one of the thousands each year which break open in the post and have to be repacked by the Post Office. This will probably entail delay, damage or loss at your expense. Often just a little extra care and attention is all that is needed to ensure a parcel's safe arrival. This leaflet provides general guidelines and gives you advice about the special packing which some goods require.

3 Specially manufactured 'slimming' foods are not necessary to lose weight. One of the most effective ways of doing this is to cut out or reduce some of the starchy foods you possibly eat too much of, including bread, cakes, biscuits, sugar, rice and potatoes. But do not reduce the protein foods, milk, fish, cheese, meat and fish, as these are needed to replace tissues as they wear. Avoid chocolate and sweets between meals which will soon put the pounds on again. Ask your doctor, health visitor or nurse for some recipes for slimming foods.

4 Whenever you leave home, make sure that all the doors and windows are properly secured — don't forget the garage.

If you are going out for the evening, leave a light, but not the hall light, switched on.

If you are going away for a few days, stop the newspapers, milk and any other deliveries. Be sure to make the arrangements in person or by letter — don't leave notes for a passer-by to read.

Leave a key with a trusted neighbour and ask him to keep an eye on your home for you. Take jewellery, silver and similar articles to your bank for safe-keeping.

If you will be away for a longer period, also tell the police.

5 Take steps to warn other drivers of an obstruction. If your vehicle is fitted with hazard warning lights, use them. If you carry a red warning sign (a reflecting triangle), place it on the road at least 50 yards (150 yards on the hard shoulder of motorways) before the obstruction and on the same side of the road. At night or in poor visibility do not stand at the rear of your vehicle or allow anyone else to do so — you may obscure the rear lamps.

6 A deep depression approaching from the Atlantic will bring heavy rain and gale-force winds to western coasts in the early evening or later in the night. Showers now affecting eastern counties will die out temporarily but rain will spread from the west during the night reaching the London area and the south-east soon after dawn tomorrow. Temperatures are likely to remain constant.

7 The Town Hall, which is on the south side of the main square, facing the Cathedral, dates from the fifteenth century. It has a fine early-Renaissance courtyard which can be reached through any of four archways, one on each side of the building. Notice the dramatic stone carvings surmounting each archway which represent memorable scenes from the early history of the town. Do not miss the magnificent wall-paintings in the Council Chamber, parts of which are attributed to a pupil of Tintoretto.

8 Is your hair limp, lifeless, unmanageable?

Do you envy other women with soft, shining, lustrous hair that every man (and every other woman) turns to admire? They've used Golden Glamour conditioner which gives their hair that loving care and gentle nourishing tonic that creates radiance and new beauty.

Why not give your hair that glow of health that really sophisticated women have achieved together with the breath-taking loveliness it is waiting for and deserves?

9 A report we have just received from Southern Amalya suggests that yesterday's attempt to overthrow the government there has met with only limited success. The rebels have been evicted from the Presidential Palace, which appears to have been one of their main objectives,

though they still control the radio station and the airport, both of which are said to be surrounded by loyalist government forces.

We hope to be able to broadcast further details in our next news bulletin in two hours' time.

10   If you wish to claim for loss or damage to an item, we ask you to complete our form P58, which can be obtained at any post office, and to return this (together with the certificate of posting, or a photo-copy where appropriate) to your local Head Postmaster. We aim to acknowledge all written claims within a week of receipt and to resolve claims relating to the inland postal services within 6 weeks.

11   Authors' alterations cost money and cause delay.

In fact every alteration or addition means laborious and therefore costly work for the printer. If printing costs are increased, the publisher's chance of making the book pay is reduced because he must either raise the price or sell a larger number of copies to cover expenses.

The object of this booklet is to demonstrate the cost of making a number of typical alterations. Authors will appreciate that it is to everyone's advantage if they make their alterations while their work is in typescript and not after it is set in printer's type.

12   I have to admit that I found the whole production well below his usual standard. The idea of a contemporary 'Macbeth' is far from original and in this case achieves nothing at all in interpreting the deeper themes of the drama. The acting may well have been influenced by the dreary costumes and setting: it lacked vitality, interest and significance. Some settings were on the verge of absurdity. Macbeth encounters Banquo's ghost at what might have been the Annual Dinner and Dance of the Dunsinane Golf Club, held in the local Town Hall, hired for such occasions. Are there not enough deaths already in this barbaric tragedy without murdering the play itself?

13   A.V.E.C. (Electronics) Ltd. invites applications from mature sales personnel (aged 35–50) who have successful experience in marketing electrical components in countries of Western Europe for the post of Sales Manager in our newly-established production branch in Frankfurt. A good knowledge of German is essential.

Important qualities are an ability to take charge of a new and expanding sales department and to show adaptability in responding to new circumstances and challenges.

Salary is negotiable and will be made attractive for the right person.

14   Exclusive development of luxury flats now nearing completion in elevated position affording breath-taking views over the South Downs and the sea. Excellent train services to London and Brighton from local station (5 minutes by car). Bus service to town centre. Large living-room, luxury kitchen, two bedrooms, colour-suite bathroom. Gas central heating. Garage or parking space. Telephone for brochure Southminster 121212.

15   Capricorn. With Mars now passing through the sign of Neptune, you are advised to reconsider any arrangements you may have made for journeys by sea or air. Over the next few weeks you should concentrate on developing leisure activities, in particular gardening or home improvement, during your free time. There will be various obstacles to advancement in your job and overcoming these may put some

strain on your nerves and physical stamina. However a firm but relaxed attitude will finally disperse most of your problems.

16 Marley's got the ball. He's well away, straight down the pitch. Maxwell tries to tackle but Marley swerves and goes on. Mowbray is waiting; he's coming towards Marley; will he tackle? Not a chance. Marley lobs the ball to Milton who hesitates a second and then shoots. Oh, a lovely shot! Oh, what a pity! It just hit the crossbar and bounced back into play. Mackintosh, the goalie, is on to it like a flash and sends it right back to the centre. And that's the whistle for half-time.

17 Our luxurious Tri-Stars are in constant service between London and the sun paradise of the Mediterranean and the exotic Middle East.

Our Emperor Class offers all the space for cushioned relaxation an emperor himself could require, with superbly comfortable reclining seats arranged in pairs and a wide choice of the finest European and Middle-Eastern cuisine. You can tune in to the most recent films or to your favourite kind of music or just tilt your chair and dream your journey away.

Fly Suncrest, the airline that really cares for you!

18 You have told me in your rather sad little letter that the young man you have given your whole heart to has now found another girlfriend and has left you all alone. You are in despair because you are afraid you are fated to become a lonely old maid.

But my dear you are still only sixteen. You have plenty of time to meet another young man who will prove more constant and trustworthy and whom you will love even more deeply.

Cheer up, my dear. Who knows? Mr Right is probably waiting just round the corner.

19 May I have your attention, please?

The captain and crew would like to welcome you aboard. May I take this opportunity of informing you about some of the facilities available to you.

Our self-service restaurant on B-Deck is now open for a wide variety of hot and cold dishes. The bar-lounge forward on B-Deck, the tea-bar on C-Deck and the duty-free shop, which is situated just near the purser's office on C-Deck, are also open.

Money can be exchanged at the counter opposite the purser's office.

You are respectfully reminded that no one is allowed on the car deck during the crossing. You will be notified when to rejoin your cars shortly before the ship docks.

In view of the unsettled weather conditions we would recommend that you move about the ship as little as possible.

We wish you all a very pleasant crossing.

20 What should you do if your cat climbs a tree and can't get down? If a dog, child or another cat has chased him up the tree, remove the offender from the scene. Then put some strong-smelling fish (boned) or cat food at the base of the trunk and call the cat by name. If he has a special bowl in which you place his food and recognises the sound of his food being prepared, create the same sound for an extended length of time, using his special bowl. This will make him hungry. If he fails to respond, go away for a half hour. He will most likely come down all by himself.

Structured communication exercises

Advice

This last part of Paper 5 could involve any of the following activities:
— responding orally in a given situation
— eliciting information by question and Yes/No answer on given subject areas
— offering definitions or opinions on specific objects
— problem solving by the discussion of various situations described or pictured
— talking on a briefly prepared topic leading on to a more general discussion
— discussing one of the set texts (if you have studied one)

You may be tested individually, or you may be expected to take this part of the oral examination with one or two other candidates (according to how your examination centre wishes to conduct the interviews).

This means that it is essential that you practise speaking English as much as possible in order to feel confident and relaxed about talking in front of other people. Don't worry about their criticisms: all they are thinking about is what to say next.

Also practise the following activities in class, criticising each other in the way you express yourselves and discussing how you can more effectively organise what you say.

Remember that only a limited amount of time can be spent practising speaking in class however, so try to seize any opportunities that present themselves for speaking English outside the classroom.

If these never occur, talking to yourself in English can be a surprisingly useful activity.

Exercises

Situations

What might you say in each of the following situations?

1 Your television, which is under guarantee, is not working properly. Telephone the firm responsible for repairs, mentioning the guarantee, explaining what seems to be wrong and fixing a time when someone can call and see to the set. There will be some difficulty in arranging this as you are normally working during the day.
2 You have sent a registered letter to a friend in another country. Four weeks later you hear from your friend that the letter has not arrived. You take the receipt to the post office to make enquiries. You will be asked by the clerk how you know the letter has not arrived, what it contained and how the contents were wrapped inside the envelope.
3 You think you have left a pair of gloves on the bus so you go to the local Bus Depot to make enquiries about them. You will be asked to describe the gloves, and to say at what time and on what bus they were left.
4 As a tourist in Britain, you are enquiring at a tourist office about somewhere to stay the night. You will be asked about the kind of room you want, approximately how much you are willing to pay and where (in the town centre or surroundings) you would prefer

to stay. There may be some difficulty in finding a room for you.

5 When looking for a book as a present for a friend, you remember one that you are sure he or she will enjoy. You know the name of the writer but cannot think of the title of the book. Prompted by the bookseller, you explain the situation and give some idea of what the book is about.

6 Something quite unexpected is going to prevent you from going to work for a day or two. Telephone your boss early in the morning, explaining what has happened, asking for time off and suggesting when you will probably be able to return.

7 You wish to travel in a week's time from London to Vienna by train and boat. You are asking in your local travel office about routes and times of trains, whether there is a second-class sleeping-car on the train, how you can book a sleeper for the night of travel and finally the return fare and the cost of a sleeper in one direction only.

8 You are staying in a London hotel and wish to join an organised sight-seeing tour. You ask at the hotel reception desk about tour possibilities, prices, the places included and length of tour and times and places of departure.

9 Your present vacuum-cleaner makes far too much noise, refuses to absorb dog's hairs from your carpet and is too large to get under low shelves and cupboards. Ask your local dealer about other possibilities, including prices, guarantee, and demonstration arrangements, if any.

10 Your very unpleasant cold has lasted a fortnight and though you are still carrying on your job, you feel tired, depressed and far from well. You finally consult a doctor, explain what is wrong, ask for advice and also whether you can have a medical certificate to allow you a few days off work.

11 You have arranged by letter to stay with a British family as a paying-guest but at the last minute have to postpone your departure, owing to some kind of strike. Telephone the family to explain the situation and suggest some alternative travel plans or other arrangements you are considering.

12 You go to a travel office to get some information about a place where you can spend your next holiday. You describe the kind of holiday and place you would enjoy and ask for some suggestions.

13 Your ten-year-old son has gone out to play and has now been away for five hours without coming back for his dinner. It is getting dark. You report the details to the police, who will want a description of the boy.

14 A close friend has been having trouble with his eyes for which the specialist says that there is no treatment available. Someone gives you the telephone number of someone who is said to have had the same trouble and been treated successfully. Telephone the person, explain the situation and ask for details.

15 In the corridor you meet a friend who has just returned from a Mediterranean cruise. You are both rather busy but there is enough time to ask about whether it was enjoyable, accommodation on the ship, places visited, fellow passengers and/or similar matters.

16 You have noticed a couple of men who seem to be paying undue attention to the house of a neighbour at present on holiday. One of them is actually looking through a window. You telephone the local police station, explain the situation after giving your name

and address and are asked various questions about the men.

17 You are reporting at the police station the theft of your car. The police want details of time and place of the theft, and a description of the car. They ask you whether it was locked.

18 You are discussing with the secretary of a language school the type of course you would find most useful during the coming session. You are asked about your standard of English, what you hope to get out of a course and the evenings you would be free to attend.

19 You are telephoning a theatre box office to ask whether you can transfer a seat booking to a later date as you find you will be unable for some reason to attend on the evening in question. You will have to give details of your existing booking and will then discuss the possibilities that are still available.

20 You intend to stay in a certain town for six months and are consulting a local TV hire firm about TV rental possibilities, the kind of sets that are available, renting terms, minimum rental period etc.

Eliciting Information

In pairs, student A thinks of a famous person and student B asks questions to find out who it is. Student A can only answer 'yes' or 'no'.

Example: Is the person alive or dead?
 Is / was the person male / female / Danish / an actor?
 Does / did he / she live in Brazil / China?
 Does / did he / she have 12 children / a bad reputation?
 Can / could he / she speak several languages / sing?
 Does / did his / her name begin with F / P / Y?

Other categories you could use are:
a country; a large town; a film; a book; a type of food; an animal.
  For further practice, think of your own categories.

Definitions and Opinions

a) **Choose one of the following and describe it, thinking about: shape, size, colour, weight, what it is made of, what it is used for.**

Items: a suitcase; an envelope; a roller skate; a calendar; a chair; a mouse; traffic lights; a cup and saucer; a thermometer; a hammer.

b) **Give your opinion of the following, thinking about whether:**
— they are useful or not
— you like or dislike them
— they are practical or not
— they are safe or dangerous

Items: racing cars; the cinema; cigarettes; animals as pets; Coca Cola; motor scooters; holidays; circuses.

When you have practised with these items, think up some more for yourselves.

Problem Solving

Say what you would do if:

i) you had your wallet or handbag snatched from you in the street
ii) after having a meal in a restaurant, you discovered you had left your money at home
iii) you wanted to find a good private English language teacher
iv) you missed a train and had five hours to wait for the next one
v) alone in a house and in bed, you heard someone moving about in another room.

Talks **Prepare a talk on one of the following topics, and then be ready to answer questions and have a discussion on it:**
  i) your ideal holiday
  ii) the most beautiful part of your country
  iii) the worst film you have seen recently
  iv) private cars should be banned and everyone should ride bicycles
  v) men should take part in beauty contests.